Chisel, Mallet Plane & Saw

Making Furniture by Hand

Tony Konovaloff

Drawings by Judith "Obie" Konovaloff

Chisel, Mallet, Plane and Saw

Making Furniture by Hand

Published by Tony Konovaloff, Cabinetmaker
Oak Harbor, WA 98277
www.tonykonovaloff.com

ISBN: 978-0-615-61877-7

Library of Congress Control Number: 2012905238

For Benjamin, Jeremiah and Caleb
Should any of them choose to follow this crazy path for a future....

And for Tory, Muff and Missy
Friends now gone

About my only regret is not getting this done before my Dad passed away....

Thanks

Like just about any book, there are a few individuals that deserve to be singled out and thanked. Without them this book would not be what it is.

Sooz, my wife - For just putting up with me on a daily basis

Pop and Obie - For everything

Tom Chartier - For friendship, enthusiasm and my Stanley 45

Paul Alt - For constant reviews of sloppy rough drafts that lacked drawings and the frequent letters with questions

John Brown - For questions, a pull no punches attitude, his own work and writing and for believing in the value of hand tools and the work created with them

Jim Krenov - Who was more of an influence than either of us will admit

And everyone who has ever bought or valued my work

I can teach a man to sail but I can never teach him why.

Timothy E. Thatcher

Start of the Book
Say So

There are no shortcuts in learning to use hand tools. It takes time and a lot of hard work. You could read every book ever written about them and might be no further ahead than the guy who just picked up the tools and tried them out. This isn't to say that books and articles are of little use. Much of what I learned early on came from books and magazines.

But it reaches a point where you have to close the books and pick up the tools. Whether you are setting up a plane or cutting dovetails, using the tools to try something will teach you more than any written word. Even mistakes teach very valuable lessons.

Also, a lot of this book wouldn't exist if I had done only what was found in books. I had little to no direction or instruction for many of the methods I write about. At times all I had was a vague picture or idea and every thing branched out from that point. Maybe this is why apprenticeships at the turn of the century were so long. Experience is a teacher not easily dismissed.

Why Hand Tools?

I wish that I had a short, concise and comprehensive answer to this question but, I don't. While I may not be able to teach you why you should work with hand tools, I can give you some good reasons for doing so.

I think the most important one for me is that I enjoy it. Whenever I do something with my hands there is a sense of accomplishment and satisfaction that just can't be achieved by other means. With hand tools there is no doubt that the results are directly related to my labors. Whether it's the time taken or the quality of the results there is no mistaking just who has done the work. Besides, there is no tired like a tired you have earned....

I am very comfortable with the pace of hand work as well. Working by hand allows me to carefully look at wood prior to cutting or think through some complex joinery without a change of pace. The steady and regular pace of working this way allows me to do better work.

The environment that hand tools create could not be better. There is very little dust or noise in my shop. I don't need a respirator or hearing protection to safely do my job. And the chance of injuring myself or my kids in the shop has been drastically reduced and in some cases eliminated altogether.

Hand tools have become a sign of quality unhurried, reminiscent of a time when very different attitudes prevailed. And while slavish devotion to the past is not good, a solid base of knowledge of the ways of the past does create a foundation for better work.

Marching to a Different Drummer

I really care about what I do; not only in the end result but also in how it gets done. In today's fast paced, almost out of control world you do not hear of too many people who love what they do for a living. While I don't make a lot of money the pay back comes in other ways. And what is so bad about making less money doing something you really care about? The things I make might be for others, how I make them is for me.

I have never wanted to be one of the crowd and working by hand does set me apart. At the present time I don't think there are more than a handful of people in the industrialized world who do furniture work entirely by hand. Part of me would like to see this change.

What's in this Book

What I have tried to do with this book is tell you how I do things without leading you by the handtool. It is not about every way possible to do things rather it is my way of working. My way of making carcase furniture, dressers, hutches, break fronts, blanket chests and the like. Sorry, I haven't made a chair as of yet so I would not presume to tell you how to make one.

You will find that this book is organized from a common sense perspective. It starts out in the shop with your woodpile and roughly ends with putting finish on. There are a few more things after this but it made sense to me to put them where they are.

It assumes some prior knowledge about the tools and methods discussed and requires some trust in what I have to say. At the same time, don't disregard what you may already know just because I say otherwise.

If you are going to work with hand tools I think you will find something of worth in this book. It is in your face and opinionated and I accept sole responsibility for that.

Cabinetmaker

Contents

Ars Longa Vita Brevis

Hippocrates

Tools, Workspace and Wood

Tools seem a logical place to start and when I look back on things, it just may have been a tool catalog that got me into this in the first place. For myself, handtools hold a certain attraction. Maybe it's what they stand for or possibly holding on to a part of the past, I cannot say for sure. I just know that I like the tools and what I can do with them.

rip and crosscut saw, jackplane as a scrub, 1/4", 3/8" and 1" chisels, jointer plane, 15 tpi backsaw, plow plane, marking/mortise gauge, folding rule, square, scratch awl, mallet, coping saw, spokeshave, block plane

Not a very long list, but here is almost nothing you cannot make with these tools. In fact, I had even less than this when I made my first piece of furniture 25 years ago and half of that was borrowed.

This is not to say that you should handicap yourself with such a small kit of tools but this does form the basis for what I call core tools. Once you have a good kit of core tools, add to them when you find a need. Do buy the best you can, as you will only end up replacing anything that isn't. Also, don't let the tools dictate what you are going to make. Decide what you want to do with your tools and get the tools that enable you to do that.

Old Tools or New

Most of the tools in my kit started out as new. I don't have any thing that is unusual or not available somewhere (well maybe one or two). All in all, there are a good percentage of new tools available that are of very good quality. Taking a look through any number of catalogs will surprise you with just what is available in traditional woodworking tools.

I am not infatuated with old tools for the sake of their being old. The main advantage of old tools is their price. As long as the tools you're after are not rare and collectible you can find some decent buys at garage sales and junk shops. Just be very cautious and certain of what you are buying.

Sometimes though you have to head in the direction

of old because that is all that is available. The idea that older is always better is a myth. But there are exceptions, such as old Disston handsaws and the quality of some older laminated plane irons. I think the main reason older tools have this reputation is that some one has cared for and taken care of the flaws so you end up with an already tuned up tool. Many of today's tools just need a bit of attention to work just as well if not better than your Grandfather's tools. And there are new tools available that are much better made than even the best of cared for older tools, but they will cost you an arm and a leg.

Workspace

No matter what type of work you do you need to have some place to work. I have worked in a lot of different shops, all with their own peculiarities. My first shop was not really a shop at all, it was the backyard. I have also worked in barns, back bedrooms, a loft above a chainsaw shop, a basement, garage and a shed I built. My shops have been located in my house, right outside my house and some of them were several miles away. If nothing else these shops have shown me just what I am looking for in the ideal shop.

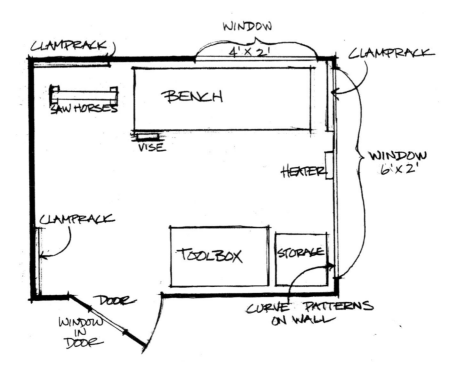

A Place to Work

You don't need a lot of space to make things. One shop I had was extremely small, at only 65 sq ft but I still managed to make anything from small boxes to China Cabinets. Most people found it hard to believe I worked in such a space. While it was a little small it did provide a place for me to keep making things. And a small shop is better than no shop at all.

Even though I have worked in a lot of places there are several things that, at least for me, are a necessity for doing decent work. Good light is mandatory; plenty of windows that face the right way are my preferred light source. Skylights are nice just make sure they don't leak.

Wood floors are a must; concrete and tile are just too unforgiving on your feet and to dropped tools. Lastly, some sort of heat in winter, A/C if needed in summer and wood storage right in the shop. While this has not always been the case, it has been my desire to have such things.

My Current Shop

The one car garage at my house currently serves as my shop. The best part about it is that it's more than three times the size of my old shop. It is just about the ideal size, but not quite. I wish it was a tad bit larger, to provide more room for finishing and working on a new piece at the same time. But this shop does have room for wood storage, which I have not had for a long time. Having the garage door to open in good weather is a nice feature and makes it convenient to restock my wood supply. Easy access to the house is nice as well. A bench for my boys keeps them off my bench, but allows them to be out with me and doing their own thing.

For the first time I am able to have a dedicated sharpening and metalworking bench along one wall. This is a real benefit, if you have the room, as it keeps metal and wood in separate areas. I used to sharpen things on my wood bench, which was not easy or convenient in the middle of a project.

Like all my shops though I will make changes as I find the need to. Recently, I covered the floor with 3/4" tongue and groove plywood so I no longer have to work directly on the concrete. Someday I am going to cover this with solid wood flooring, but the ply will get me by for now. I want to improve my window situation next, and then find a better way to seal the roll up door while still allowing it to open.

A Word About Small Shops

As many of the shops I have worked in show, you can work just about anywhere and still get things done. Even the kitchen table will work, but don't blame me if your significant other doesn't like it. At one time I even used to stack wood in the hallway of our house. All you really need is room for some sort of workbench and a few tools.

One thing I learned very early on is that everything has a place if you are going to work in a small shop. I keep mine very neat, much to the consternation of my wife; I am still less than neat when it comes to the house.

I started out in a space quite a bit smaller than the one I am in now and that first shop shaped a lot of my work habits. I had to be picked up and organized because there was not room to be a slob. It's the only way I could work in the lack of space I do. And in all honesty, I prefer the intimacy of a smaller shop. Everything is close at hand and that small space is cheaper to heat as well.

The layout of my shop evolved with my work habits and your shop should do the same. What works for me won't necessarily work for you.

Selecting Wood to Use

Wood is such a varied and different material my only words of advice to a

hand tool woodworker are to use wood that works well with your tools. Alder, Walnut, Cherry and Pine are all pleasant to work with. All of them plane easily, are not a problem to glue up and are readily available. Some are harder than the others, but they all are tool friendly. By no means do I limit myself to just these, I also work with Big Leaf Maple, Oak, Teak, Mahogany, Douglas Fir, Pear, Manzanita, Makore, Sapele plus many others.

The tools by nature impose some restrictions so don't handicap yourself further by using wood that's mean to your tools. Woods such as Teak and Rosewood can be worked by hand, as cabinetmakers of the past proved, but they are hard on your edge tools. Nor does it help that I am allergic to Dalbergia, the family of trees that make up all the types of Rosewood. They can also be a problem to finish not to mention the problems of the forests they come from. They are obscenely priced as well.

Most of my wood is kiln dried from a local lumber supplier. I tend to buy surfaced lumber, as there is little benefit to buying rough lumber when you have to plane it by hand. Not to mention the fact that you can't even see what you are getting with rough lumber. The wood I buy is only surfaced on the faces and the edges are still rough. All the mill marks come off as I make a piece anyway. The kiln dried versus air-dried is kind of a useless argument unless you are building boats and need the bending qualities associated with non- kiln dried wood. They both have merit so use the wood that works for you.

One last thought about buying wood. Be picky. Just because the lumberyard may have bought some junk doesn't mean you have to. If the yard does not want to let you pick through the lumber go somewhere else. At the same time though, be reasonable in what you expect from the yard, don't expect them to unstack thousands of board feet of lumber so you can pick out a few sticks. Buying wood requires some give and take from both sides.

Wood Storage

After messing with numerous shops I have come to the conclusion that I prefer vertical storage to stacking things up. I have found that standing boards up makes it easier to sort through them, which I do frequently, and takes up far less space. The only restriction on storing wood this way is the height of your shop. I had to punch out some sheetrock in mine so now the boards go up into the attic space. Do provide some way to prevent your stock from leaning over and falling on you or one of your projects. The rafters take care of this in my shop. Take a look around at your local lumber supplier to see how they do it.

Alder, A Personal Favorite

I stumbled across Red Alder back when I first started making furniture and wanted to move on to hardwoods. I have made blanket chests, dressers, china cabinets and all sorts of other furniture with it. Unfortunately, you are not very likely to find it if you do not live in the Western part of the United States.

Often it is bypassed at the lumberyard as a lowly paint grade secondary wood which is a shame as kiln dried stock has a warm orange brown color when oiled. Air-dried stock has a much more orange color and is prone to what someone described as "watermelon stains". These are large splotchy white areas throughout a plank. I have also been told this can occur if boards are not put into the kiln soon after cutting.

Alder's grain is subdued, but can be lightly figured and prismatic. I have even come across a piece covered with bird's eye, which is extremely rare. I have only seen it once in the couple of thousand board feet I have worked with or sorted through over the years. Small knots are common, but these only add character from my view. One other thing I have run into is small mineral deposits. These are greenish in color and tough on plane blades. One swipe and there will be a good size nick in the blade. Watch for them and plane around them and over them only during the last few passes.

It holds screws well; glues up without a hitch and handplanes leave a surface that is almost glossy. When paring end grain there is a tendency for the wood to crush if your chisels are not absolutely sharp. Taking light cuts will help. Another plus is it's availability in my area, most lumberyards carry it.

About the only down side to this wood is it's movement in use and difficulties in finishing. Contrary to what the books say personal experience has shown that it moves a lot, as much as 1/4" in 12" of board width, winter to summer, and this is a finished piece of furniture, in a centrally heated home (mine). As long as you are aware of this you can build to accommodate it and avoid problems before they occur. Alder can be difficult to finish as well. I use a lot of linseed oil/wax mixture and when first applied the wood appears "cloudy", but this clears up in a couple of days. I have no idea why, but it does.

All in all with it's subdued grain, easy workability, and pleasant color, Alder is my favorite wood. And remember, if you don't like it, you can always turn it into chips and smoke a fish with it....

Thoughts About Cutting Trees

        As a woodworker I am the direct recipient of products from the forest so I am partly responsible for trees being cut down, but this doesn't mean that every tree standing should be brought down. Cutting apart a tree is always a gamble, you never quite know what you are going to get until you make those first cuts. Trees are wonderful things whether they are providing shade or cut into pieces of lumber. I love wood, but sometimes it's better left in the tree....

Saws and Sawing

Sawing is really pretty simple, push and pull with a jagged piece of steel. But I have to admit there is a bit of a dance involved when cutting things up as a lot is going on between you, the saw, the horses and your stock. It takes awhile to find a balance to make it all work, but in the doing you will find what does and does not work for you.

I can't say enough about the importance of having sharp saws. Most people have never even used a sharp handsaw, and maybe this accounts for the surprised looks I get when I tell people I cut up everything by hand. A sharp handsaw is a joy to use and a dull one is a nightmare. For me the best saws are old Disstons, at least when it comes to crosscut and rip saws, even some old English woodworking books say this and it is still relevant today. Somehow Disston figured out the perfect balance between hardness and ease of sharpening. I got my old Disston's from my grandfather's garage. They were wrapped up in 20-year-old newspapers, all sharp and ready to go. Like someone had just gone to the sharpening shop, picked them up and promptly forgot about them. I have also had good luck with saws made by E. C. Simmons under the Keen Kutter brand name.

Rough cutting the parts for a cabinet does not require a lot of tools, a crosscut and rip saw, marking tools and some sturdy saw horses. After doing a lot of this I am ready for a nap. This is also why I cut things up when nothing crucial has to be done later.

Before You Cut Things Up

Most importantly, take your time deciding on how and where you are going to cut things up. Do whatever it takes to make sure you are cutting wood up just where you want. Pencil marks or chalk can be very helpful. Mistakes at this point are extremely frustrating. While you may get away with gluing a ripped board back together, once you crosscut a piece there is no going back. Board stretchers haven't been invented yet.

Be ruthless when it comes to saving offcuts. Hang on to pieces of a reasonable size but use restraint, as it is very easy to accumulate a large pile of almost useless scrap. Dusty boxes of offcuts are better suited to the fireplace.

Another thing to keep in mind is to not cut up any more wood than you need at the moment. You don't need to cut out drawer stock before you have even made the carcase. Pace yourself, cut pieces out as you need them.

Saw Horses

After sharp saws, the only other things you really need are a couple of stout saw horses. You might get by with less than the best quality when it comes to saws, but sawing up stock on wobbly horses is frustrating at best and could lead to your kids learning some new words.

The best way to look at sawhorses is to think of them as a workbench for your saws. They don't need to be fancy as you will hit them with saw teeth now and again, but they have to be sturdily built to prevent any motion. I nailed together a pair more than 20 years ago and they are still with me.

A quick and easy way to get the height is to stand up, bend one leg and the distance from your knee to the floor is a good working height. This allows you to hold down your stock with a knee and get your saw started or move your stock around with your free hand. This height is also handy for working on a partially completed cabinet. Keep some carpet scraps around to act as padding when using your horses this way.

Cross Cutting

First remove a short section on the end of your stock to eliminate checks, then use a pencil or chalk to mark your lengths. Always start the cut by pulling the saw backward while using your thumb as a guide and keep your cut as close to your sawhorses as practical. Your saw is more efficient when there is support right next to the blade.

Make sure to plan for the inevitable splintering that will occur on the backside of your stock. Depending on what you are cutting and how important that backside is you may want to flip your stock and cut from the back side. Or you might even want

to go to the trouble of scribing a knife line to prevent the splintering from affecting the piece you want to keep.

Don't forget to support the offcut as you get to the end of a cut or it will tear out a chunk as it falls, and that chunk will more than likely be on the piece you want to keep. I just reach across the saw to hold the offcut. For stock too heavy or awkward to hold I have a stool that serves as a third saw horse.

Never force your saw to work. If anything other than light pressure is needed to make your saws work, it is time to head to the sharpening bench.

Find a comfortable pace and let your saw do the work. Never hurry, as this is when you are most likely to put a kink in the blade and they are difficult to remove at best. This brings up another point; never loan your saws to anyone. It is just too easy for someone to damage your saws beyond repair.

Ripping

Ripping involves some careful planning and coordination to avoid cutting your sawhorses in half. This doesn't mean you can't tag the edge of the horse once in a while but you want to avoid it if possible.

At least one straight edge on your stock is needed to mark out for ripping to width. I rough out a square and straight edge with a scrub plane and finish it up with my jointer plane. You need this edge as a reference for a panel gauge.

A panel gauge is just a marking gauge with a long beam and an oversize fence. Mine has the capacity to mark out a panel up to 26" wide. You will probably have to make your panel gauge just as I had to make mine. When setting your panel gauge, don't use a tape measure. The loose end could create minor errors. I use a 24" bi-fold sparmakers rule that I found in a junk store.

Once marked for final width with my panel gauge, I cut the board. There is an old adage that applies to both ripping and crosscutting (or any hand tool process for that matter) "cut on the waste side and leave the line". Leaving the line allows for some clean up as rip and crosscut saws don't exactly leave a finished surface.

Start the cut just like crosscutting, by pulling your saw backward and using your thumb as a guide. You may need to do this more than once to get a kerf established. Once there is enough of a kerf to guide the saw you can move your thumb.

Make sure to have some shims nearby in case the kerf starts to close up and bind your saw. Slip the shim into the kerf a bit away from the saw and this will keep

the kerf from closing on the saw. The shim should be a bit thicker than the kerf left by your saw and you may have to keep moving the shim along your kerf. A bar of paraffin rubbed on the sides of your saw can help with a binding blade as well.

Try to keep the saw cutting as close to the horse as you can as this prevents the stock from springing and robbing efficiency from your stroke. As you begin the cut, the saw is outside the sawhorse, when you have enough kerf move the saw between the horses. Don't hesitate to use the entire blade. You paid for a whole saw so utilize it.

When you get to the end of the cut slow down so you don't cut into your sawhorse. Finish the cut with the waste side hanging off the edge of the horse or push the end of your workpiece off to the side with just the corner on the horse and this should give you enough clearance to nick off the waste.

Cutting Curves

Curves take a little more care to cut than a straight line and they also require a different type of saw. A Bow saw makes quick work of the curves I use on my work. It has a narrow blade (only 3/8" wide) that is tensioned by a wooden frame.

Bow saws take a lot of practice to learn to use. Mostly this has to do with the narrow blade of the saw. Unlike crosscut and rip saws, the blade of a bow saw likes to wander from your line.

When cutting curves it is very important to cut a clean line. Your rough-cut curve needs to be as close to your finished curve as possible. The reason for this is that a curve is far harder to "move" than a straight line and it is also more difficult to finish up the edge when it has a curve cut on it.

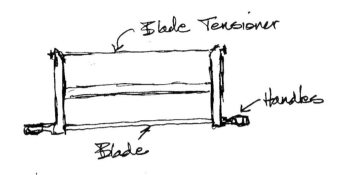

Blade Tensioner

Handles

Blade

The main thing that is different from cross cutting and ripping is just where I make the cut in relation to my marked line. I find it much easier to follow a curve by cutting directly on my line. The "leave the line" adage doesn't apply to curves. The narrow blade is harder to control than the wide blades of crosscut and rip saws; so slicing right down my line has been very effective. I make sure that my marked line is just a bit wide of where I want the final curve to end up. And I find the best way to mark my desired curve is to make a pattern.

To get better control of my bow saw I almost always place my workpiece in my face vise using the saw in a horizontal position. This way I can concentrate on following my line and not on holding the board down.

Resawing

I enjoy working with hand tools, but I am not a glutton for punishment. So, needless to say resawing is kept to a minimum in my shop. It is bordering on crazy to take a piece of 8/4 stock and slice it into thinner pieces by hand when 4/4 stock is so readily available. If you are after book matched panels that's another story. I am not

saying that you can't do it, I have. If you have to do a lot of it though, it will wear you out beyond belief.

To make resawing a pleasant experience there are a few things you can do to help. Don't resaw more of the stock than you need, shorter pieces are much easier to deal with. A sharp rip saw is an absolute must. Stay with softer woods if possible and keep the stock you are cutting up fairly narrow, 5" to 6". Very hard or dense woods should be even narrower. If your stock is very wide, you may want to consider ripping it in two prior to resawing. Then glue it back together after you are finished sawing.

Set a marking gauge a bit fat of the thickness you want to end up with. This bit of extra accounts for the kerf removed by the saw and allows for clean up. There will be quite a few saw marks to remove and some of them will be rather deep.

Run the marking gauge around the edges of the board. Make sure to use the

13

same face to mark all four edges. I don't worry about the edges being too smooth unless I need to make the scribe line more visible. And even then, I only knock off the fuzz or waney edge with a scrub plane. Generally, a scribe line is visible even on rough sawn wood.

I use my face vise to hold the workpiece. I tip it away from me and start the kerf by cutting right on my line. Be sure to cut from both sides. If you try and cut it from only one side you can't see if your saw is wandering from the scribe line. And by cutting right on the line there is no guessing which side of the line you are supposed to be cutting on as you turn the board around.

As you get deeper into the board you may need to slip some shims into the kerf. And when you reach the last part to be sawn this is a must. Clamping the board in your vise, right on the shim will hold things open so you can finish the cut.

When all is said and done, my hat is off to the pit sawyers of yesteryear...

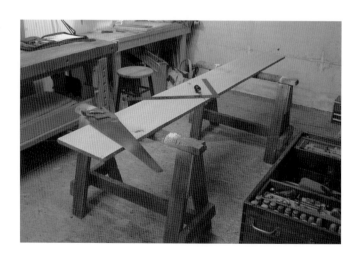

Workbench

Your bench is the largest tool you will own and it is very important to your shop. Whatever you end up using to work on, it directly affects the results you are going to get. You don't have to work on a masterpiece of craftsmanship, but there are several features that I feel are essential to a suitable bench. It should be heavy, have a flat, stable top, a rigid base and a face vise that will securely hold anything you put in it (within reason).

I am of the mind that what's on your bench is more important than the bench itself. This is not to say you can't have a really nice bench, but when you have to use backing boards to avoid scratching the surface of the bench things have gone too far. For me the bench is the backing board. I don't mistreat my bench, but it has its place in the order of things.

There are also many stops and fixtures that are part and parcel to how I use my bench and in the following paragraphs I will go over them in more detail.

Work Surface

The top of my bench is a big hunk of wood that stays put. It is made of Douglas Fir 2 x 4's glued face to face so I ended up with a bench that was, at one time 3 1/2" thick. Initial and periodic flattening has reduced this by about 3/8".

I prefer a softwood bench as it is a little easier on dropped items and Douglas Fir is not as "slick" as a hardwood bench. Another plus is that Douglas Fir is extremely stable.

Just how big to make your bench top is a matter of personal preference. My bench went through an evolution of sorts, being cut down in length and width several times to accommodate changing work habits and different shops. I eventually ended up with a 73" x 27" work surface. And while I am happy with the width, at times I wish it were a bit longer. If I ever get a larger shop, I will probably make a new top that adds a foot or so to the length.

I keep the top of my bench well oiled with the same oil and wax mixture I use on my furniture. I wipe the top, once or twice a year, with leftover oil from furniture projects. This keeps stains and dirt from embedding into the surface and the wax in the oil keeps glue that drips onto the top from sticking.

Keep It Flat

Your bench top should be relatively flat but it won't stay that way. No matter how well it's made, your bench is going to move with the seasons. Check for flatness at the same time each year or you will find yourself chasing the movement. Also make sure to check it after it has a chance to stabilize to a new shop.

Flattening a bench is not difficult. For the most part it is just a large exercise in planing. When planing check frequently with a straight edge and winding sticks so you don't compound an existing problem. See the chapter on Handplanes for more on winding sticks and how to flatten a surface.

The Base

The base of my bench is built solidly to prevent rocking or any other motion. It is made up of 4x4's that have checked pretty heavily due to the fact I used green lumber and did not allow them to dry properly. But this doesn't seem to have had any effect on it.

The base is an integral part of how my bench is used. There are holes drilled in the legs that hold fixtures and dowels to make many jobs easier and more efficient. And along these same lines, if you use a pencil quite often you will find the back of a front leg is an out of the way and convenient place to keep a pencil sharpener.

Remember to build the base as a separate assembly from the top. The legs should never penetrate the surface of the top. I found out why, the hard way, when I first made my bench. Changes in humidity will shrink and expand the thickness of the top while the end grain of the legs stays stationary. The legs will first rise above the surface and then go below it. Depending on the material of your top and your weather this could be a major nuisance. And needless to say I eventually made a new base frame that corrected this problem on my own bench. Mistakes teach lasting lessons....

The height of your bench is important. Don't think bench manufacturers have the perfect height worked out either. You have to find a comfortable working height for your work habits. I set the height of my bench by standing up and measuring from the floor to the back of my wrist. This put my bench top 34" from the floor and I haven't found the need to alter this in the 23 plus years I have been using this bench. Experiment to find what works for you. Don't be afraid to alter the height with blocks or a saw.

The Vise

       One thing that has been a great time saver for me is the type of vise I have fitted on the front left corner. It is called an instantaneous bench screw and takes it's name from the fact that it only takes a quarter turn of the handle to lock or unlock. There are no threads and it has to be seen to be truly appreciated. About the only way to get one is to haunt the junk shops and yard sales. I got mine in a trade from a friend more than 25 years ago. Come to think of it, it may have been the first tool I obtained.

       Screw type vises are entirely suitable; just make sure you get one with a quick release feature. The quick release will save a considerable amount of time.

       The other type of vise I have fitted to my bench is a twin-screw face vise that is actually on the back side of my bench. This vise is made up of two pieces of threaded rod, a few nuts and washers and a 4 x 4. The threaded rod is fastened through the

back edge of the bench. Two holes in the 4 x 4 allow it to slip onto the threaded rod and two large nuts attach it to the bench. The 4 x 4 serves as one jaw of the vise and the bench serves as the other. Primarily I use it when dovetailing carcase pieces. There is 28"

between the rods so it will hold any carcase piece I am ever likely to put into it. Since it crosses the full width of a carcase side, it keeps the workpiece from rattling around when sawing on the end grain.

I learned to make things without a tail vise so I do not have much use for one. I think they are given an unearned place of importance, but I would not remove it if my bench were fitted with one. For the one time I do find a tail vise helpful, I came up with an alternative made from a couple of blocks and a pipe clamp. This vise is quick to set up and easy to store when I am done with it. See the Carcase Joinery chapter for a photo of this set up.

Stops

I use a variety of different stops on my bench. The one I use the most is just a small piece of Elm that slides in a mortise through the top of my bench. The Elm is tough as nails and the mortise is cut a little small so the stop gets tapped with a hammer to move it. I prefer wood stops over metal because sooner or later you are going to plow into that stop and I would rather hit a chunk of wood with the plane or blade than a metal stop.

For wide boards, panels or carcase sides I use a panel stop. My panel stop is made from a thin slat of maple screwed to a 2 x 2 block. The block gets clamped in my face vise and the end of the slat is C-clamped to the back edge of the bench top. This creates a stop that crosses the full width of my bench. Clamp a couple of stops on the back edge to prevent sideways movement of your workpiece and you are ready to start planing.

Screw type hold-downs are helpful for attaching stops and blocks to aid planing and lastly a large screw run into the top of the bench right next to the edge. This screw/stop enables me to work on boards right along the edge of the bench, mostly when I cut rabbets.

Fixtures

I have several fixtures for my bench. A bench hook is a must have. I just knocked one together from scrap I had laying around. It gets used for cutting small pieces to length, cutting shoulders on tenons and as a substitute shoot board for small pieces.

A support board fitted with dowels that fit into the holes in the legs of my bench is mostly for edge planing, but has other uses as well, such as setting hinges or drilling edges of boards. A board jack sees it's share of use supporting long boards and a small vise mounted bench is handy for planing small workpieces.

More Info

The Workbench Book by Scott Landis will tell you more about workbenches than you ever want or need to know.

Handplanes

There is one thing at the heart of making things by hand. And that's the need to learn to use planes. Almost everything revolves around your ability to use them. This includes not only your skill in using them, but also the know how to set them up in the first place.

There is a myth that has persisted for a very long time and almost everything you read about handplanes continues to pass it along. This myth is about the traces that handplanes leave behind. The truth of the matter is that handplanes, when set up and used properly, leave no tell tale trace of their passing. There are only a couple of ways to tell if a hand plane has been used on a flat surface and that is if it was set up wrong in the first place or the time wasn't taken to prepare it for use. The only other way would be if the plane was intentionally used to leave marks. Such as using a flat soled plane on a curved panel.

I have been planing surfaces for over fifteen years now and you will not find evidence of my planes having been there. Unless of course you consider smooth, clean, and flat surfaces proof of handplanes. And no, this is not achieved by sanding or scraping. I gave up on sandpaper at the same time I picked up handplanes and I use scrapers only sparingly because scraped surfaces generally need to be sanded.

When set up properly and used with care and attention to what you are doing, perfectly smooth and flat surfaces, glueline free joints and assorted other tasks are easily accomplished with a handplane.

Metal or Wood

I mostly use iron planes with the few exceptions being a couple of specialty planes. I like the stability and the feedback you get from a hunk of iron. It seems like you would get a lot more feel from a wood plane, but that is just not the case. If you are comfortable with wood planes, by all means continue to use them and while much of the following still applies you will have to adapt some of it for it to be of use.

About my only complaint with iron planes has more to do with the makers of them than what they are capable of. Just look at every new plane as a kit not a finished product and you won't be half as mad. What this means is that you are going to have to do some work to get the most out of them. So I figure the best place to start is how I go about preparing them. The following pretty much applies to all metal bench planes.

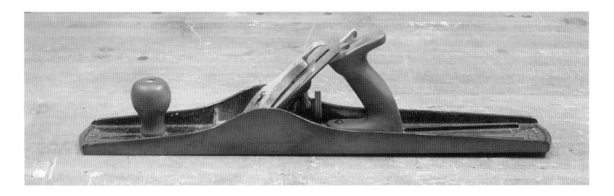

Preparing Planes

Use a straight edge and square to check for flat and twist. Most new planes are not. If you do get lucky, don't mess with a flat sole, just put it to work.

To flatten the sole, first place sandpaper on a known flat surface. 1/2" tempered glass makes a good flat surface and is not too expensive about $15 for a 8" x 30" piece. Don't hesitate to start with coarse paper and use roll type sandpaper not pieced together sheets. I use 80 grit to start. Most planes are ground at the factory with 60 grit. If you start with finer grits you will be there forever.

I leave the frog and blade tightened into the plane with the blade backed out. Run the plane back and forth on the sandpaper, using firm, but not excessive pressure and check progress frequently.

You can work your way into finer grits, but don't forget the goal is flatness not polish. I go no further than 120 or 150 grit.

Take a file to all sharp corners of the plane body, the factories used to be much better at this. Also, remove the finish from wood handles and replace plastic handles. This is not a philosophical decision; rather the aforementioned offenders will give you blisters.

Setting Up the Plane for Use

I use a Stanley No 7 for virtually everything. It is big and heavy, but I have gotten used to it because it does such a great job. There are things it is not good for, such as smoothing and cutting chamfers, and in these situations I use a different plane. The following section mostly applies to my No 7, but where appropriate I will let you know about things to do differently with other planes.

Placement of the Frog

I use a small throat opening, about 1/16". This is a good middle of the road setting as I use my No 7 for many tasks. Smaller and it jambs and bigger results in tear out. If you need a much different setting, grab a different plane. You will find tinkering with the frog is a pain.

Sharpening the Blade

If you can't shave hair easily the blade is not sharp. What you want to end up with is an almost straight blade that feathers out at the edges. This is easy to achieve with the natural wear of oilstones or just apply pressure at the sides of the blade during honing.

A convex edge (1 to 2 thousandths) makes any bench plane work better and is a must on a smooth plane. The curve eliminates the corners digging in and makes fixing twist on edges and narrow pieces easy. It also helps to remove unwanted bevels or put on ones you need. One other note: I keep 11 blades ready because I hate to stop in the middle of a task just to sharpen blades.

Setting the Cap Iron

A set back of about 1/32" works in most situations. You won't get chatter with an even larger set back. I have only seen chatter when trying to take too heavy of a cut, a loose cap iron or a board not secured properly to the vise or bench. If you have a hard time believing me on this one consider the lowly block plane, it does not even have a cap iron....

Set the Blade

Most books will tell you to hold the sole up to a light source to set the blade. Don't. Hold the plane by the sole with your hand cupped over the throat and the heel of the plane on your bench. Sight down the sole and use your other hand to adjust the blade. The sole needs to face a light source and wear a dark shirt. Trust me on this last one, as it is an immense help.

The Lever Cap

Prior to tightening up the lever cap, while it's still loose, pull back on the blade to ensure that it's tight against the adjustment levers. When tightening down the lever cap it will tend to force the blade farther out the throat. So, lightly snug up the lever with what appears as too little blade showing and pressing the lever all the way home should give you the desired blade setting. Remember, when setting the lever cap, it should start to snug up before it runs out of room.

How to Hold It

First of all, there is no right or wrong way to hold your planes, but how you hold them can affect the results. Hold firmly, but don't strangle it.

For edge planing, I hold the rear handle of my No 7 with my forefinger extended out to the blade or frog and with my other hand, I wrap thumb and forefinger around the edge of the plane next to the knob. In use, the back of your forefinger touches the workpiece and acts as a sensor and guide to help control the plane.

For surface planing, the grip is almost the same with the exception that you now use the front knob for obvious reasons.

Using Your Planes

Having a plane set up this way allows you to concentrate on using it, not on how to set it up for the upcoming task.

Start planing by knocking off the high spots with short strokes and moderate pressure on the plane. To oversimplify things, a surface you are going to plane is nothing but high and low spots. A concave surface is high on the edges or ends and a convex surface is high in the middle. Twist is no more than high spots on opposite corners. Even a rough surface fits this definition, as it is nothing but lots of little highs and lows. Whether you are working a flat surface or a perfect edge joint, planing is about removing these high spots.

And it goes without saying that you should almost always plane with the grain not against it. Running your finger along your stock will generally tell you the lay of the grain, even on some smoother surfaces. And if there is not a distinct grain direction, the board will plane better in one direction than the other.

Pay attention to what's happening; even watch the throat of the plane to see where shavings are coming off the blade. You will find you can pinpoint spots you want to remove just by shifting the plane left or right. Bevels are a good example of this. You can remove or add one simply by using one or the other side of the plane sole. The left side of the plane removes the right edge of your stock and vice versa. But this will only work if the blade is sharpened with a slight curve. That slight curve in the edge also helps blend plane strokes together on flat surfaces.

When using your planes, try to develop a rhythm and flow and stay balanced. Keep your body as close to your plane as practical with your arms firm, but not locked and use your legs. Planing uses your whole body not just parts. Throwing the plane with your arms will tire you out and give you sore elbows from stopping the momentum of that hunk of iron.

Don't be afraid to take a few swipes on the sole with paraffin, it makes the plane easier to push and can even give you a few more passes with an almost dull blade (try it if you do not believe me). As for the wax will wreck the finish argument, it doesn't interfere with the oil/wax finish I am partial to and remember, don't coat the sole, just a swipe or two. And the one plane I do this only sparingly to is a smooth plane. You will know when the high spots are gone when you get even width, full length shavings from your work piece. Low spots show up a s a break in the shaving. Final passes should run the full length of your stock. And keep a straight edge and winding sticks handy to check your progress.

Flat Surfaces

Often the first thing you will have to do to a board is flatten one side of it. For the most part this is very simple; just knock off the high spots until the stock is flat. One word of caution here: Don't get carried away with "flat". Wood will always move and if you are not careful you may find yourself chasing an unattainable perfection.

Minor imperfections are not going to be a problem. I will leave it up to you to define minor.

If the stock is close to flat you can knock off the high spots with your jointer plane. If it is way out of flat you need a plane with more bite. I use a scrub plane to rough out a flat surface or to clean up a rough edge prior to edge jointing. A scrub plane has a flat sole and a blade with a convex edge. It leaves a rough fluted surface, but removes stock quickly.

Setting Up a Scrub Plane

A No 5 jack plane makes a good scrub plane and they are probably the most common plane lying around unused. All you need to do is grind a blade to shape and

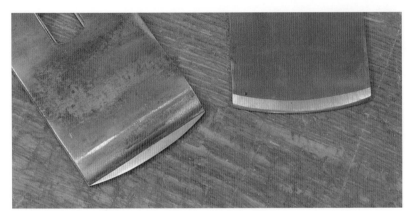

move the frog all the way back to open up the throat.

To make the curved edge, grind down the corners by about 3/32" then pivot the blade to shape your curve. You will find that it is easier to grind a curve than a straight edge. This amount of grinding should give you about 3/32" of blade beyond the cap iron at the center. You don't need more than this because it's hard enough to plane off even a 1/16" thick shaving.

Using a Scrub Plane

I use my scrub plane to cut with the grain, diagonally to the grain or, with caution and a sharp blade directly across the grain.

To flatten and thickness-plane a warped or twisted board, I first scrub equal amounts of wood off the high spots on one side, and ensure it is flat by sighting across winding sticks and planing until the sticks are parallel. (Following paragraphs go over winding sticks in more detail). And lastly, finish up the surface with a jointer plane.

Setting the Final Thickness

I scribe a line on all four edges to mark the desired thickness of the board, using the just flattened side as the reference for the fence of the gauge. Then I scrub off this side to the line and joint it flat. When removing lots of wood like this, I plane with the grain and diagonally to it. First remove a layer with the grain then switch to diagonal to remove the next layer and so on. This helps to maintain flatness when removing lots of stock and it also gives you a visual reference of just where the wood is coming off.

It will take numerous passes to remove a large amount of wood and lots of effort on your part. Planing directly across the grain is usually reserved for wild grain that just won't plane any other way.

When planing a large panel, the blade can get hot, so I am careful where I lay the plane. To keep the blade cooler and to avoid dulling it, I don't drag the plane blade back over the wood before taking another cut (this applies to all planes...). I also knock dried glue squeeze-out from glued up panels before I thickness-plane and smooth them. I use the side and leading edge of the plane body and not the blade to do this.

Making and Using Winding Sticks

Winding sticks are two matching pieces of wood used to check for flatness, twist, alignment, etc. You will need to make your own, as I don't know of any tool supplier who sells them. Dimensions are not critical; they are chosen to suit the maker. Mine are only 18"L x 1/2"T x 1 3/8"H (each). Anywhere between 16" and 24" would be a good length. Even longer "sticks" should be used for flattening large tables or a workbench.

Any stable wood can be used but a darker wood will make them easier to use and also allow you to put sights into them. Sights are just small pieces of contrasting wood inlaid near the ends of one of the sticks to improve visibility during use. I made my sticks out of Ebony and made the sights of Tagua nut.

After you have chosen your stock, true it up square, then clamp it together with two small C-clamps. Plane the long edges to ensure that the pieces are parallel to each other. This is what makes the sticks work; it is essential that the sticks are identical or at least as close as you can get them.

While the sticks are still clamped together mark one outside corner on each piece, then remove the clamps and chamfer the corners you marked. This chamfer ensures you use the sticks in the same position you made them in.

Sights and Finishing

I inlaid small squares of Tagua (vegetable ivory) into the top edge of one of the sticks on the opposite side of the chamfer. These squares, 3/8" x 3/8" x 1/8" thick, are placed about 1/2" from each end. In use the sights make any irregularities much more apparent.

There is nothing but a light coat of oil on my sticks for a finish. A coat of paste wax would work just as well. Do not use a glossy finish, as the glare will make them hard to use.

Sticks in Use

Winding sticks are very easy to use. First remove any cupping from one side of your stock, place the sticks at opposite ends of your workpiece, the one with the sights farthest away from you and the chamfers should be facing in opposite directions. Step back a pace or two and sight across the top of your winding sticks. If they line up parallel you have a flat workpiece, it not you have twist that needs to be removed. Also be sure to check the entire surface for flatness by repositioning your sticks along your workpiece. Plane off any high spots and be sure to work on opposite corners to remove twist. If you only work on one end you will have a flat surface that feathers out on one end. When your sticks line up the entire length of the stock you have a flat surface.

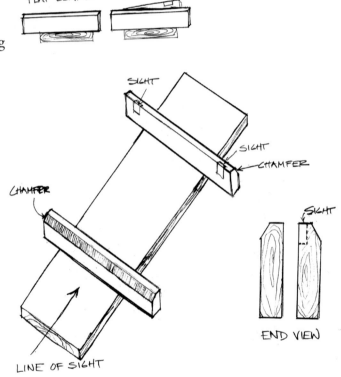

Edge Planing

If there is a "Zen" to woodworking, this is where it will manifest itself. Nothing quite compares to the feel or "click" of a perfect edge joint coming together. There is no trick to edge planing just patience (of which I have none) and paying attention to the task at hand. A No 7 is not a magical cure all, but how you use it can be. First of all don't bother trying to edge joint two boards at once, yes it can be done, but all you have to do is try to put those two boards back into the vise to make a correction to the joint and you will see why I don't like it.

Set the blade to take a light cut, also make sure the blade is absolutely sharp. Too heavy of a cut will not make things faster, only more difficult. Rough in the edge with a scrub plane. This plane will take the brunt of the wear and you won't have to sharpen your jointer irons as often.

28

As you work the edge start with pressure at the toe and gradually shift the mild pressure to the heel at the end of the stroke and remember, the entire edge is a single stroke. Only use short strokes to knockdown high spots. The final passes are continuous from end to end.

When the edge "feels" right get out your square and straight edge and see how you did. For long pieces a six-foot level is a good inexpensive straight edge and it may also tell you if there is any twist in the edge (the level will rock). Double check twist with a square it could be the level. For very long (5 feet and up) and wide (more than an inch)

edges and stock that is less than flat, winding sticks are a much better choice. They won't tell you if it's flat in length but they will quickly identify any problem areas that are difficult to locate with a square. A long board with a slight twist may check out with a square when the edge actually has a twist to it. Winding sticks will quickly and easily show you where the edge needs to be worked. Don't fret if things are not as they should be, practice is the cure.

Once you have that first edge done match the mate to it. One step leads to

the next. The end result of all your labor should be a joint with no visible glueline. If it still shows you haven't done it right.

Remember, you can't force the plane to work properly. If frustration sets in, put the plane down and come back to it later. Frustration will only make this a bad experience. Edge planing not only takes the proper tools, but also the proper mindset.

Shooting End Grain

Shooting boards are popular with some people and they work well with small stuff, but get into larger work, large panel or cabinet sides for example and they are not very practical. Most of the time I shoot end grain instead of freehand planing. This ensures it's square and true, but I don't use a traditional shoot board. Rather, my bench becomes one with stops and blocks clamped to it. This method is far more flexible, than a conventional shoot board, and easier to store when you are done with it.

Set Up Your Plane

The sole must be flat with square sides and the blade set square to the endgrain you are going to shoot. If you sharpen blades with a slight curve as I do set the blade to take a square cut where the stock contacts the blade. The lateral adjustment lever of an iron plane will compensate for a slightly out of square sole as well.

One other note, shooting endgrain takes a much heavier setting of the blade compared to surface or edge planing. Set the plane up right and you will pull off shavings not just dust. Don't forget to file off any sharp corners on your plane, as doing a lot of this will give you blisters in rather odd places.

Set Up Your Bench

Clamp a 2x2 stop block to the back edge with a hold down or C-clamp with the end grain facing the front of the bench. Every once in awhile I use a second stop to the left of the first one to better stabilize my work piece. Use two equal thickness scraps to elevate your workpiece. This raises

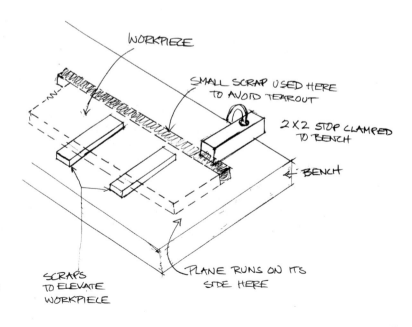

WORKPIECE

SMALL SCRAP USED HERE TO AVOID TEAROUT

2X2 STOP CLAMPED TO BENCH

BENCH

SCRAPS TO ELEVATE WORKPIECE

PLANE RUNS ON ITS SIDE HERE

it above that small section on the sole of the plane where there is no blade exposed. Place a back up scrap between the block and workpiece to prevent the back edge from blowing out. Lay your plane on its side and have at it.

In Use

Using your plane this way will dull one section of the blade quickly, but don't put it aside or resharpen right away. By varying the height of the support pieces you can utilize the entire blade before heading back to your sharpening stones. I usually start out with thin spacers to use the lower half of the blade. Then, after this dulls out, I use thicker spacers to enable the upper part of the blade to be used. Make sure to use the lateral adjustment lever to get a square cut on your stock.

This set up works great for almost any size workpiece and is indispensable when squaring up pieces too long to stand up in a vise. Don't forget that a bench hook can be used in a pinch on small pieces when you don't want to drag out all the blocks.

Block Planes

Find a block plane that is light in weight and put in a better blade than the one that came with it. I put a Hock blade in mine. I have also heard that the blades in Lie-Nielsen planes are some of the best made.

I have an old low angle Stanley that I would not part with. It has the wrong shoe and there is a chip in the sole but it's perfect for how I use my block plane.

Mostly I use my block plane to cut chamfers. To make this more efficient I angle the blade in the plane. One side takes a heavy cut and the other a finish cut. When doing a lot of chamfers this saves quite a bit of time.

Are low angle planes worth it? Don't quote me, but I would say that blade quality has more to do with good results than the difference in angle. So find one that is comfortable in your hand, haunt the junk shops to find an old one cheap.

Something to think about when planing a lot of endgrain, grab a larger plane. I have often seen the advice about how well a block plane works in this situation and while this is partly true, a larger plane works even better.

Smooth Planes

One of the reasons I ever got into using hand tools stems from the fact that I hate the scratchy sound, mess and throw away mentality that goes with sand paper. The surfaces I can get with a plane are much "cleaner" and smoother than sanding will ever achieve. Another great thing about smooth planes is that it is much faster to

plane a surface than to sand it, I don't have to keep working up to the next grit or worry about leaving things in the finish, as the only thing applied to the wood is a sharp piece of iron.

I set up my smoother, a Stanley No 4, with a very small throat and the cap iron set close to the edge of the blade. As with my No 7, I keep a few extra irons ready (4) and they must be extremely sharp. I always finish honing on a Hard Black Arkansas to get the finest edge I can.

There is not all that much I can add to using a smooth plane that several hours spent using one will not teach you. That and following the advice I offer up in the first part of this chapter. I think most problems that occur with planes are the result of not preparing the plane for use and setting it up poorly. The quickest way to learn to use a smoother is to get yourself a piece of pine or other easily planed wood and have at it. Once the plane is working well, stop and take the blade out and force yourself to re-set the blade. The ability to set up the plane consistently is the most important thing in learning to use this or any other plane.

One little trick that can really bring out a nice surface is to burnish the freshly planed surface with shavings. At first I did not think just rubbing a surface with shavings would do a thing, but I gave it a try and it can bring out a little extra on a planed surface. One thing to note though is that this will not save or make up for a badly finished surface. You have to start with a nicely planed surface to begin with and remember to get the shavings off your bench not the floor.

Rabbet Planes

There is not much of a trick to setting a rabbet plane. Just make sure that the blade takes an even shaving and the blade extends slightly past the side of the plane. If the blade does not extend out the side, the rabbet will start to get narrower with each pass. The amount of blade sticking out should be a little heavier than a shaving and your plane will work just fine.

Shoulder planes are a little tougher to set, but this is more of a sharpening dilemma than a set up problem. Because the blade projects from both sides of the plane body the blade must be absolutely square. I

think most problems with a shoulder plane are caused by an out of square sharpening job. By keeping the cutting edge absolutely square to the sides of the blade during the sharpening process you should not have any problems. Using a honing guide makes this much easier. Also, don't hone a curve into the cutting edge. Rabbet plane blades need to have a straight edge to work properly.

Combination Planes

At first glance Combination planes are quite the contraption. But looks are deceiving as these planes are very easy to use and extremely valuable to the hand tool cabinetmaker. They are the best tool going for cutting grooves and dadoes.

While Combination planes can be used for a lot of different tasks, for the most

part I use my Stanley 45 as a plow plane and dado plane. Setting it up to use as a plow plane is the same as any other plane, but there is also a fence that must be used. When setting the fence take care to ensure the fence is parallel to the body of the plane.

The only thing I do differently when cutting a dado is to turn the spur cutters so they will cut the edges of the groove and prevent tear out and to make sure the blade does not project past the spur cutters. The spur cutters are little blades that nick the grain just ahead of the main blade. This way the main blade doesn't lift the edges of a dado causing tearout. Most of the time when cutting dadoes the fence is not used; rather a thin batten is tacked on to my work piece to guide the plane.

Also when cutting dadoes in a carcase piece I tend to cut the rabbets for a back panel first and then cut the dadoes. After the first pass or two, I use the shallow dado as a guide for my backsaw to cut down into the dado. This prevents the plane from blowing out the back edge at the rabbet. Cutting the dadoes first would prevent the need for this but I never seem to cut the dadoes before the rabbets

Spokeshaves

Setting up a spokeshave is not any different from setting a plane. The only difference is that the adjustments are made with a different mechanism. You still want a razor sharp blade with a slight curve to it and a setting that takes a fine shaving.

Due to the extremely short sole of spokeshaves, be careful that the front of the sole doesn't dig in to your workpiece. Use a light touch to prevent this and check your progress frequently to ensure that you are keeping the curve fair and not digging a hole.

Spokeshaves are not the easiest tools to use, so don't get discouraged if things don't go well at first. Keep at it though and you will be surprised how often you reach for this overlooked tool.

Scrapers

As I mentioned at the start of this chapter, I do not use scrapers all that much. This is not to say that I don't have any, there are three types I use. Flat steel scrapers of different thicknesses come in very handy at times. The ones I use are made by Sandvik, they hold an edge well and come from the factory almost ready to use. I also have what's called a cabinet scraper, which is just a flat scraper mounted in a steel body. The only time my cabinet scraper got a lot of use was when I needed to level out the boards on the floor of one of my shops. The other type of scraper I use is a one-inch wide hook scraper. This is a rough tool mostly used for removing dried glue or scraping mineral deposits so they don't tear up a plane iron. It is sharpened with a file while flat scrapers need to be honed on all sides.

The one time I find scrapers essential is when I remove the excess wood that sticks up after I glue in stringing. The scraper takes off the excess without damaging the surrounding surface. When sharpened properly and used with caution, I can get away with not having to replane the surface.

Chisels

A chunk of steel with a sharp edge and a piece of wood for a handle. Tools for working wood do not get any more basic than this. Chisels are not that hard to learn to use and learning to use the proper chisel for the task at hand is simple as well.

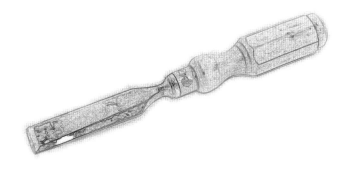

Chisels are a good example of getting what you pay for. Cheap ones are not worth your time. Most of the time they will not hold an edge, which is the worst thing possible in a chisel. Spend a little extra on a quality set and you will not be disappointed. I have had good luck with Footprint and Sorby chisels, both of which are made in England.

Types of Chisels

There are many different types of chisels, but the ones you will find the most use for are beveled edge Bench chisels, Sash Mortise chisels and Registered Mortise chisels. Bench chisels are primarily for paring with hand pressure and mortise chisels are made to withstand the heavy pounding from a mallet. Bench chisels can be tapped with a hammer, but they should be the "hooped" variety to avoid splitting the handle.

I cannot over emphasize the importance of sharp chisels. Sharp chisels are necessary for any kind of accurate work and dull chisels are dangerous at best. A sharp chisel is easier and safer to use and gets better results. A good way to check for sharpness is to pare a little bit of endgrain and look at the surface left by the chisel. If it is not smooth and burnished, your chisel could stand a bit of attention. (See the sharpening chapter for more). Mortise chisels don't need to be quite as sharp as bench chisels, but it does make them more efficient. I do tend to let them go longer between honings even though I know better.

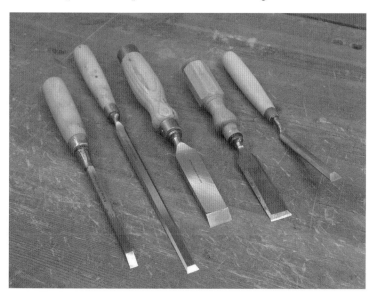

Be sure to keep all chisels away from nails,

screws and any other edge nicking material. It doesn't take much to destroy, at least temporarily, a perfect edge.

Specialty Chisels

There are several other types of chisels that you will find beneficial. Some of them you can buy and others you will have to make yourself.

Pattern and Crank-necked chisels are just variations on bench chisels. Pattern chisels have long thin blades and crank-neck chisels have a bend at the handle to get it out of the way when paring in the middle of a board or other awkward location. I have the 1/2" size of each.

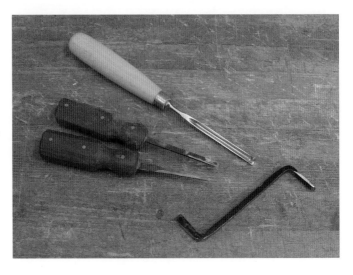

A 1/4" In-cannel gouge is extremely helpful when setting hardware that has curved edges. Unlike a carving gouge the bevel is on the inside of the curve allowing you to chop straight down with ease.

I have two small chisels that I made for working on keyholes. One is a 1/16" mortise chisel and the other is a very thin, flat 1/4" bench chisel. Two other chisels that are a good idea to have are, a 3/8" bench chisel ground down very thin and a Lock mortise chisel. The thin 3/8" chisel finds it's way into narrow gaps of some dovetails and other narrow spots that most chisels can't reach. The lock mortise chisel has two 90-degree bends to enable you to get into some awkward locations that no other chisel can reach.

Using Bench Chisels

I place a lot of importance on using chisels. Dexterity with a chisel is a skill that will never let you down and it just may get you out of a tight spot when no other tool will do the job.

While there are many quality chisels available, the Sorby paring chisels I use have an advantage over most other chisels; they are fitted with "London Pattern" boxwood handles. In my opinion there is no better shape for a paring chisel handle. These are much better than the typical round handles found on most chisels. London Pattern handles can be held comfortably many different ways and with narrow chisels they won't roll off your bench.

The first thing to take into consideration when using your chisels is that there is not a wrong way to hold them. Some ways just work better than others. A general rule to think about is the closer your chisel is to your body the better control you will have.

The chisel has more stability this way. Sometimes I even use my chin to aid stability and to push the chisel when practical. And don't be afraid to choke up on the blade with your hand either. Your fingers will act as a stop and help you control the cut. This is really good for paring when there is no back up board to prevent blowouts.

Paring on end grain takes a little bit of care. I have a simple way to avoid tear out on the back side of a piece I am paring. I either make sure the workpiece is tight against the bench and use it as a backing board or I only cut halfway from each side of my stock to meet in the center. Also, several light cuts are better than one heavy cut, as they are more likely to cut the end grain cleanly. A heavy cut tends to crush and tear things.

An important point to remember is to never put yourself in the path of the blade. If it slipped, the only thing in its path is your flesh and you are no match for a razor sharp chisel.

As with your planes remove the finish on the handles of all your chisels to avoid getting blisters. A scraper and light sanding is my preferred method, but some of the new non-toxic strippers do this quickly and easily as well. Do tape off any metal, as the stripper will discolor it.

Mallet

Tapered Handle Slides through Head

Mallets and Hammers

I use two things to pound on my chisels. A large wood mallet for my mortise chisels and Warrington hammers for doing delicate tapping. I prefer wood mallets for heavy pounding, as they are less likely to do damage to the chisels. The face of the mallet is flat and angled to make it easier and more accurate to use. Warrington hammers make it easy to maintain control when doing lighter work and are handy when setting the blades of wooden planes. I also have a round Lignum Vitae mallet, but it is only used for working with carving chisels. The round angled face is not the best for trying to chop mortises or other precise cutting, but it is just what's called for while carving.

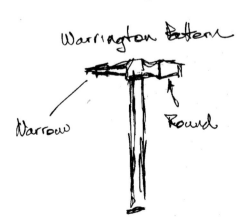

Warrington Pattern

Narrow

Round

Using Mortise Chisels

Mortise chisels are made heavy and meant to be smacked with a mallet. Registered Mortise chisels are "hooped" at the top and bottom of the handle with a steel ring to prevent splits in the handle from heavy pounding. They are used on large mortises.

Sash Mortise chisels are only "hooped" at the bottom and are used only on smaller mortises.

Mortise chisels are pretty easy to use. Line up the chisel with your marked lines, chop down and lever out the waste. When I start chopping, I always stay a bit away from the ends of the mortise. Saving some of the mortise for final fitting makes for a cleaner job that is a better fit for the tenon.

Make sure your chisel is going in straight and square to your stock. Frequently eyeball this as you get deeper into the mortise. It's easy to wander, but hard to correct. I have a tendency to lean my chisel to the right so I need to be cautious and remember to correct for this.

For small mortises, I just chop out the waste with my chisels, but whenever I am removing large amounts of stock I always take out the bulk of the waste with a brace and bit. This speeds things up considerably over just chopping out the waste of a large mortise. Make sure to use a bit that is a tad smaller than your mortise.

Whenever you have to cut a through mortise, first chop in from one side then turn your stock over and chop in from the other side. This makes for a more accurate through mortise. Most of the time I clamp my workpiece to the bench while I am working on it. Make sure the pounding doesn't loosen up your clamp. Falling clamps put nice divots in tool boxes....

Something to keep in mind is to pay attention to what is under the mortise you are chopping. You don't want to chop into your bench so you may find a backing board to be a good idea. This is about the only time I use a backing board. It's hard to tell just when you cut through, as there is not much difference between the wood of your bench and your stock.

Carving Chisels

I have not spent that much time carving and only recently have I added to a small set of carving tools. Primarily, I use these when working on knobs and pulls or doing some type of clean up. I am also teaching myself how to carve letters. I am just getting started into more involved carving so, needless to say, it would probably be for the best if you looked elsewhere for some good information about using these specialized tools. The advice I offer up on other chisels though is still valid, buy quality and keep them sharp.

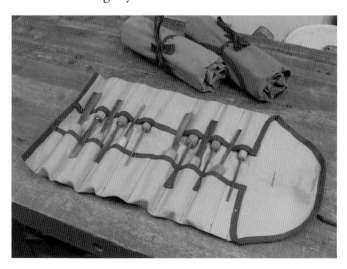

More About Carving

How to Carve Wood, Richard Butz, 1984, The Taunton Press.
    This book should get you started. It covers all sorts of carving styles.
Lettercarving in Wood, Chris Pye, 1997, Guild of Master Craftsmen Publications Ltd.
    Just the book for learning how to do just what the title implies.

Sharpening

I am not trying to glaze over this topic, but sharpening is simple; grind, hone and go back to work. I am not over fussy about how I get there, but I need to have sharp cutting edges to get anything done efficiently. How do I define sharp? If you can't shave hair easily, it's not sharp. Sharpening can be as complex or as simple as you want to make it. It can be done from a very crude level or it can be turned into an art from and I think I fall somewhere in the middle. I am pretty practical about it, as sharpening has only one purpose and that is to get me back to work.

Flattening the Back

Sharpening should start at a point that many people ignore, including me for a couple of years, and that is on the backs of your blades and chisels. Having a flat polished back is crucial to getting the best edge you can. No, you don't have to polish the entire back, but the first 3/8" or so is crucial.

Use coarse carborundum powder and water for the initial flattening and then work your way through your stones. I have found it's best to use the carborundum and water on a small steel lapping plate. Keep the mess outside and give yourself some help by using a short block of wood to apply pressure.

To keep the blade and block from moving around on each other and you, run a

screw into the block that projects a bit less than the thickness of a plane blade. Position the block so the screw comes out in the slot of the blade. Place chisels, and other small and narrow blades, to the side of the screw.

Grinding the Edge

Somewhere along the line you will have to grind blades and chisels, either after frequent honing or to make them square from the factory. I use a hand grinder. I got my grinder out of my grandfather's garage and it is a lot older than I am. I still remember cranking this thing as fast as I could back when I was 5 or 6 years old. Fortunately, it seems to have come to no harm.

There is a bit of the pat your head rub your stomach skill involved when using a hand grinder, but it does not take much practice to get used to it. There is a big plus to using a hand grinder as well, it's hard to ruin a blade due to the low wheel RPM.

I don't worry too much about getting a hollow grind as it is a byproduct of using a grinding wheel and it is not crucial to my honing style.

Something to keep in mind, I always crank my grinder so the wheel comes down into the blade. This way the heat generated by grinding tends to be carried into the body of the blade and not out on to the leading edge where it poses a risk to the temper of the edge. Once you lose that temper you have to grind past it.

Angle of grind for different types of blades and chisels
25 degrees   planes, spokeshaves and bench chisels
30 degrees   mortise chisels
35 degrees   combination plane irons

Grinding Curves

To make a curved edge, grind down the corners and pivot the blade to shape your curve. You will probably find that it is easier to grind a curve than it is to grind a straight edge. As with any grinding keep the blade moving. Don't leave it in one spot for long or you could ruin the temper by overheating the blade. Even a hand grinder moves fast enough to burn a blade.

Honing the Edge

I prefer oilstones because they are less of a mess than waterstones and with care they will outlast you. I have a coarse carborundum, Washita, Soft Arkansas, Hard White Arkansas, and a Hard Black Arkansas. These will set you back a fair chunk of change, but you will never need to replace them.

I have fixed my stones to a bench for ease of use and attached covers to keep out any dust. The lubricant I use is 100% mineral oil made specifically for honing. I don't recommend using kerosene for health reasons. I get the honing fluid all over my fingers and soaking in a solvent, such as kerosene, is not good for you. Also, kerosene will let your stones clog up faster than oil will.

One other note about honing oil. I have found that the finer the stone the less oil you need to use. This will make your stones cut much more effectively. When there is too much oil on your finer stones, your blades and chisels tend to skate across the surface.

To clean up my stones during use, I wipe them with old cotton napkins, for the most part these give up very little lint. Wiping your hands with wood shavings helps to remove oil from your hands if you need to get right back to work and don't want to leave prints on your work. Do not wipe all of the oil from your blades if they are being put away, as a small amount of oil will help prevent rust from forming.

The important thing to remember is that you do not need to hone the entire bevel. The only part that cuts is the leading edge, so I only hone the first 1/16" or so of a fresh grinding job. You can usually hone a couple of times before heading back to the grinder, so between grindings I only hone as much as I need to restore the edge. And keep a loupe handy for checking your progress, it will show you all kinds of things that your eyes alone will miss.

Work your way through all of your stones. I don't remove the wire edge until the final stone. This final stone varies depending on what I am honing whether it is a chisel or plane blade. For many of my blades I stop with the Hard White Arkansas. The finest edge is not really needed on all of your blades; so I only use my Hard Black Arkansas for smooth plane blades, shoulder rabbet plane blades and bench chisels.

Periodic Maintenance of Your Stones

No matter how careful you are with your stones they will need to be cleaned once in awhile. This is not very difficult and will prolong the life of your stones. I use a stiff brush and dishsoap in the sink. Just scrub until most of the dark residue is gone from the surface of the stones. You can't get it all but most of it will come off.

After a couple of years of use (or sooner), you will need to flatten your stones. I find this is easy to do using carborundum powder on glass with water as a lubricant. I use the backside of the glass I use for flattening planes to do this. I got my carborundum at a rock shop; use both coarse and fine grits depending on the stone you are working with.

Use lots of water and add fresh grit when it feels like it is no longer cutting. There is a distinct difference between fresh grit and grit that is shot. Use the whole surface of the glass or you will dig a hole and this will create problems down the road. A hollow piece of glass will put a convex surface on your stones not the flat surface you are after.

Plane and Spokeshave Blades

For the most part, an almost straight blade that feathers out at the edges is what you are after. Just apply a little pressure at the sides of the blade during honing or sometimes the natural wear of oilstones will take care of this for you.

Why a gently curving edge? I said it before but I think it bears repeating, a slightly curved edge makes bench planes work better and is a must on a smooth plane. The curve eliminates the corners digging in and makes fixing twist on edges and narrow pieces easy. It also helps to remove unwanted bevels or put on wanted ones.

Something else about plane blades. There can be a vast difference in the quality of blades you have for your planes. If you have double-checked your sharpening technique and it is not to blame, it could be your blades. I have had very good luck with Record irons, even though I use Stanley planes.

To make things a bit easier when honing spokeshave blades, I made a handle that holds their short blades. To make this handle, I cut a kerf into the end of a short block with my ripsaw. I just push the blade into the kerf and friction holds it in place. This gets my fingers away from the stones and gives my hands something to grasp onto. If you find the slot cut by your saw is a bit loose, use a machine screw and nut to pinch the kerf down on your blades.

Chisels and Specialty Irons

I used to think the only "true" way to sharpen chisels was using just my hands to hold the blade on my stones. Then I bought a honing guide. I bought my guide mostly for specialty irons, but it works so well with all of my chisels that I wouldn't want to sharpen them without it now. The more consistent results I get with the guide means fewer trips to the grinder, which translates to less time spent sharpening.

It is very easy to set a honing guide with a ruler or by making a guide block. This block is just a template for setting the same angle on your blades each time. I have a single block of wood with three settings for the angles I use most.

You could also make your own honing guide but I don't think it would be worth it. Buy one of the better guides available. Mine was made in England and cost around $17. Stay away from the cheap ones,

they are not made properly and chances are, they won't put a straight edge on your chisels.

When sharpening bench chisels I almost always stop honing on my Hard Black Arkansas stone. I don't do rough work with my bench chisels so having them as sharp as possible is for the best.

Combination plane irons on the other hand, need to be tough rather than razor sharp. So generally I stop honing with my Hard White Arkansas stone. This needed toughness is also why they are ground at a 35-degree angle prior to honing. Stopping with the Hard White Arkansas is also appropriate for mortise chisels.

Saws

By no means am I all that good at sharpening my saws and for me to try and tell you how to do it would be ridiculous when the book I learned from is very good and still available. The book is "Keeping the Cutting Edge" by Harold Payson and it is available from Woodenboat Publications. I do not do everything he suggests, but he definitely knows more about it than I. This book will put you on the right path.

When first learning to sharpen, use restraint, as few people are available to fix your mistakes. Most saw shops I have talked with just don't have the know how to deal with any but the most basic of saws, large tooth rip and crosscut saws. Letting them have a fine tooth backsaw could be disastrous. Ask a few questions to find out if they can fix your saws.

All that I can add to this book would be a recommended size of files list. Taper files are getting harder and harder to find, so taking your saw down to the store to "fit" the proper file is frequently no longer possible. The most likely source for taper files is one of the tool catalogs you get in the mail. By no means is this list all-inclusive, but these sizes do work for me.

Saw		Recommended File
Rip	5 tpi	7" Taper
Crosscut	8 tpi	6" Slim Taper
Panel	11 tpi	6" Double Extra Slim
Tenon	15 tpi	4" Extra Slim
Dovetail	20 tpi	4" Double Extra Slim

Saw Sets

I have two saw sets, one is for coarse tooth saws and the other is for finer toothed saws. If you want good results you will need both sizes. My saw sets are both of the "plier" type.

Be careful when using a saw set. If you try and set a tooth opposite from the way it already goes expect the tooth to break off. My ripsaw is missing a tooth because I learned this lesson the hard way.

Saw Vise

I found an old iron Sargent saw vise in my grandfather's garage and while you may not be so lucky, they are frequently available at stores that sell old tools and other junk. The other route is to follow the instructions given by Payson in his book and make your own.

Scrapers

Sharpening is critical in getting the most out of any scraper. While a file will put a usable edge on any scraper, if you want to do more than scrape paint you will have to polish up the edge of your scraper on your sharpening stones. The edge must be straight, true and polished, and the first 3/8" of the flat sides must be polished as well. This is the only way to get your scraper to cut cleanly enough to avoid the use of sandpaper.

After polishing is finished, you can create the hook that does the cutting by making a few passes with a burnishing tool. My burnishing tool is an old saw file that my great grandfather ground off the teeth and polished up years ago. That's another point to consider, your burnisher must be polished just as well as the edges of your scraper. If it's not, it will leave minuscule nicks in the freshly burnished edge.

Furniture by Hand

This is the best part about handtools, using them to make something. From watching my woodpile get smaller to final fitting some dovetails, the use of handtools

lets me enjoy each and every step along the way. But I have found that much of what I get from handtools cannot be explained with words. I would liken it to describing a sunset; something is invariably lost in the translation. You simply have to be there, to do the work with your own hands and experience it for yourself.

Hands to Work

This part of the book is about putting the tools to work. It covers just about all the types of joinery I use and how I put a piece of furniture together.

There is a bit of a running joke that all furniture, even chairs in an odd sense, are just boxes. You start with a large box and fill it with smaller boxes (drawers) and flat boxes (doors). This says to me, when viewed from the right perspective, furniture is not that complicated to build. As long as you keep things simple and build a solid foundation of knowledge about carcase construction you can make just about anything.

When you make things by hand you provide the power as well as guides, limits, tolerances, stops, calibration, etc. Much of this is intuitive. In the doing you will learn how tight to make a joint or how smooth to plane a surface. Just how perfect things should be will be left up to you. And there are different levels of perfection....

It takes patience, dedication and commitment to make things by hand. And you have to love doing this, for sometimes there is no other reason to do it. And don't forget, nothing happens fast.

Carcase Joinery

All of my cabinets pretty much follow the same steps from start to finish. Make up the sides, cut the joinery to hold it together, cut a rabbet for the back panel, divide up the case with dadoes for shelves and drawers, glue up the main carcase, make and glue in the crosspieces for shelves and drawer blades, slide in the shelves, assemble the drawer blades, make, fit and glue in the back panel and lastly attach the base frame and any other trim pieces not already in place. While this may take a lot longer to do than to read about they are the basic steps I always follow. This section of the book goes over these steps in more detail

Slab Side Construction

For myself, the quickest and most efficient way to make things is with slab side construction. It is a simple and clean way to make things and it appeals to my sensibilities of construction and design.

Slab sides just means that all four sides of a carcase are each made from a single slab, either one piece of wood or several edge glued pieces. Very rarely will you find stock wide enough for one-piece sides, so learning to joint edges quickly and cleanly is essential. The Handplanes chapter goes over edge planing in more detail.

Gluing up Panels

I think the most important thing to remember when gluing up panels is to always place the pretty side of a board out, regardless of the orientation of the growth rings of each board. As long as the wood you are using

is dry, you should not have any problems with warping.

At this point, don't over prep the face of the stock you are gluing together. A lot still needs to happen such as edge jointing, flattening the panel, joinery etc., so over working the face will be a waste of time. I only plane enough of the face to see the grain or color in order to get a better match.

Next on the list is to have plenty of clamps on hand prior to spreading any glue. I am not the first one to say it, but you can't have too many clamps when it comes time to glue up.

After jointing all the edges of a panel I glue it together. Panels are one of the easiest things to glue up. As with all glue ups, dry clamp to find any problem areas. Should the joint not close up with only light hand pressure, take it apart and re-plane the surfaces. Never close up a gap in a glue joint with clamp pressure.

Next, I place newspaper on the joints where they cross a clamp to avoid getting iron stains on the panel. Sometimes these stains can be a pain to remove so it's best to prevent them in the first place.

I stand up the boards on the clamps and spread a layer of yellow glue on only one edge of each joint with a palette knife. It takes a certain touch to lay on just the right amount of glue, but this is easily learned with practice. I like to have a small amount of squeeze out on both the top and the bottom. After laying down the boards and pushing the joints together I close up the clamps with moderate pressure. Torquing down on the clamps will not make a better joint and it could pop things out of alignment

If you have problems with the end of a joint slipping around just place a spring clamp or small C-clamp across the joint prior to tightening up the other clamps. After all the clamps are snugged up and the glue takes on an initial set you can remove it. If the middle of the panel is the problem you may be able to push things into alignment with wedges. Slip them under your pipe clamps prior to

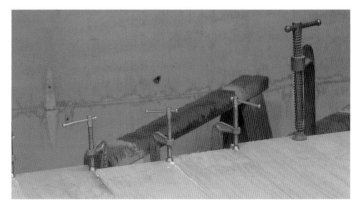

tightening them all the way. If this does not work you may have to take more drastic measures. One time I even had to have my wife stand on a tabletop I was gluing up. By the time I tightened up all the clamps she was able to step down. As for removing the rest of the clamps, I like to leave them on overnight.

Dovetails

After glue up, flattening and squaring up the parts of a carcase, I cut the dovetails to hold it all together. I still have the first dovetails that I ever cut, and they are pretty bad to tell you the truth. But I have gotten a little better since then.

Dovetails have quite the reputation, sometimes good and sometimes bad, and to say the least they are about the best way to join the corners of just about any piece of wood. They are the nemesis of many a woodworker and you are going to have to cut them well and also quick if you are going to call yourself a cabinetmaker. They are not that difficult to cut, and once you get into a rhythm they can be cut quite fast. But when first learning to cut dovetails, relax. Worry about getting things right not about how fast you can cut them, speed will come in time.

The Tails

I always cut the tails first, no good reason to; it's just a good idea to start the same way every time, as it will improve both your efficiency and your skill.

Square up your stock and set a marking gauge a bit wider than the thickness of your stock. This bit of extra lets the endgrain of the tails and pins protrude a little. Scribe all the way around each end with the gauge. This is the base line for your dovetails. Place one of your tail boards upright in your vise.

Pick a nice spacing, 2" or so for large carcases and tighter for smaller stuff. Just make the spacing appropriate to the job at hand. Set dividers to your spacing and walk off the dividers on the end grain of the tail piece.

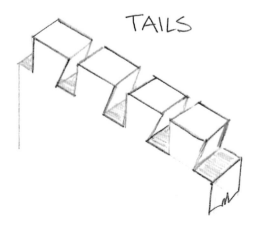

TAILS

First use your backsaw to cut down at an angle suitable for your tails. I "guesstimate" the angle and it is not as hard as it sounds, you get better with practice and slight variations in my half humble, half shameless opinion add to the joinery not take away from it. These are not large differences and there is no effort to create variations but the natural result of using hand tools. It is well worth teaching yourself to do this for the simple reason it will save time. Next, remove the waste with a coping saw just above the scribe line. Pare to this base line and you are ready to cut the pins. When paring, take extra care to keep the inside corners crisp and clean. It really makes a difference on the finished joint.

The Pins

Use the tail piece to mark out the pin board. I put the pin board into my vise and place the just cut tail board onto this. Making sure it doesn't move around, I use a knife to mark the pins directly from the tails. I cut down right next to the line with a backsaw and leave a little of the line for fitting. If you overshoot either sawing or paring of the pin, all you have to do is glue a thin shim to the pin and try again.

PINS

I use a coping saw to remove the waste between the pins. Place the blade into the kerf and just above the baseline twist the blade as you begin the cut. Concentrate on pivoting the blade before you start to cut along the line. Don't cut beyond your scribe line, as there is not much you can do to correct this. Finish up by paring to the line with a sharp chisel.

When I am finished sawing and paring of the pin board, I try out the fit. Once you get them started tap them with a block and hammer and pay attention to the sound of your hammer. It starts to ping when the joint is too tight, and this can help you pinpoint areas that still need work. Pare off the tight spots then see if the joint will go all the way together. Don't hesitate to take the joint apart repeatedly, as you really can't do any damage unless you pull the joint apart at a goofy angle.

The trick to getting dovetails apart without damage is a block and hammer. Don't try and pull a dovetail apart with only your hands, the inevitable rocking to loosen it up will damage it. Take the offending boards out of the vise. Hold the pin board up, place the block on the inside corner and smack the block, this will force the tail board out of the pins.

Once the joint goes all the way together check to see if the pins protrude past the tails. The pins should stick out just past the tail piece, plane them off almost flush so they do not get in the way of your clamps during glue up. This eliminates the need for odd clamping blocks, which tend to just fall off mid way through clamp up.

Half Blind Dovetails

Half blind dovetails are not any harder to cut and if you want to conceal some of the joinery on your work you need to learn to cut these as well.

Set a marking gauge to the length of the tails (typically 2/3 rds of the thickness of the pin boards) and scribe around each of the tail boards and across the ends of the pin boards with the gauge. Use the inside face as a reference for the gauge when marking the pin board. Also scribe the thickness of the tail board onto the inside face of your pin board, I have a second gauge set up for this step. The outer face doesn't get marked because the joints don't come through.

Cut out the tail boards the same as any through dovetails and use these to mark out the location and angle of the half blind pins. Once again, I use a mill knife to mark these lines. Once marked, you can remove the waste on the half-blind pins. Saw down the pins at an angle just short of your lines. Chop out the waste with registered chisels and pare to your lines with bench chisels.

Be extra careful when fitting as you not only have to fit the pins but the endgrain of the tails needs to fit right up against the socket you cut in the pin board. Make sure they are not too tight or they will force open the joinery around the pins.

Some Things to Keep in Mind

When all is said and done, but prior to glue up, plane off all the exterior scribe marks. Some people think it's OK to leave them, I don't, it looks like crap. Don't plane off the interior marks as it will only mess with the fit and they won't show after glue up anyway.

When deciding on the layout of my dovetails, there are some rules I always follow. When dovetailing an upright carcase, the top and bottom pieces are the tail pieces with the pins cut on the sides to keep the cabinet from spreading. It probably never will but I still make things this way.

With exposed joinery, the tails are always on the front, I feel this is the only way that looks right. On drawers, the sides are always the tail piece because the force of opening and closing is opposed when made this way. If the glue ever failed the drawer will stay together as long as you leave it in the case.

When dovetailing drawers, I always plan for the groove for the bottom panel to exit in a tail. This ensures that it does not show once the drawer is complete. Also, you have probably read somewhere that you should always end or start with a half pin, while this is sensible, there are always exceptions to the rule and for me carcases are one place I make exceptions, as I always end the dovetails at the back of the carcase with a half tail because it makes the rabbet for the back panel easier to cut.

Cutting the Back Panel Rabbet

Prior to glue up, I cut a rabbet on the back edge of all the case pieces with a rabbet plane. The rabbet plane I use for this is fitted with a fence and a depth stop.

The width of the rabbet is set by the thickness of the back panel and generally I make the depth just over half the thickness of the carcase side.

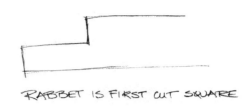

RABBET IS FIRST CUT SQUARE

Next, I bevel this rabbet with a shoulder rabbet plane, somewhere between 5° and 8° is sufficient. I do this by eye; with practice you will find it very easy to do. This bevel makes it possible to get a piston fit for the back panel. But more on that in the section that covers the back panel.

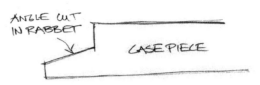

ANGLE CUT IN RABBET

CASE PIECE

BEVEL IS CUT WITH A SHOULDER PLANE

Dividing Up a Carcase

I divide the case for shelves, dividers and drawers by cutting dadoes (3/4" wide by 1/4" deep) with a Stanley 45. I used to use a backsaw and router plane to do this but it was tedious and time consuming. The 45 makes things much faster and you end up with a cleaner result.

After setting up my 45 and removing the fence, I tack a thin batten onto the carcase side to guide the plane. I use small nails to do this and I just re-use this batten at each dado. Often I use a knife to assist the spur cutters with the cross grain so there is no tear out at the back and edges of the dadoes. Cutting down into the back edge of the dado with a backsaw is helpful in preventing blowouts as well.

Glue Up

As always, dry fit and dry clamp your joinery. This will help you spot areas that could be a problem during glue up. Make sure you have plenty of clamps, a hammer and block of wood to pound a stubborn joint home and go bars to pop a carcase square. And remember, the simpler you make glue ups the better off you are.

Pipe clamps are very handy and a heck of a lot cheaper than bar clamps and they are also much easier to extend when gluing up large carcases. As long as your pipe clamps are threaded on both ends you can make longer clamps with only a pipe connector to connect the two pieces of pipe.

When gluing up a large piece, the glue may start to set before you get the case all the way together and the hammer and block can remedy the situation before it gets critical. I have even considered using a glue with a longer open time than the yellow glue I currently use, but I haven't done this yet.

Enough Glue and Square Carcases

Don't go overboard with the glue. Use only enough glue to give yourself a little squeeze out. Work like a madman to get the corners closed up before the glue starts to set up. Don't over clamp just close up the joints with moderate pressure. Wait a few minutes for the glue to take on an initial set and remove the clamps. Well cut dovetails don't need the clamps left on and leaving them in place can be detrimental. Unless the clamps are placed and tightened with the utmost of caution you can force a carcase or drawer out of square or even force a "bow" into the tail piece with too much pressure from the clamps. Eliminate the problem by removing the clamps after the glue starts to set. As I mentioned earlier, now is also a good time to plane off the protruding endgrain if there is any. This will

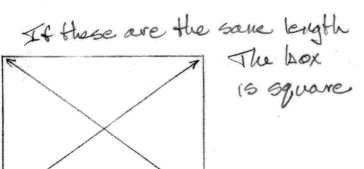

If these are the same length
The box is square

56

"consolidate" the endgrain.

It's important to check for square at this point. To do this I measure the diagonals of the box, door, or drawer I am gluing together. I use a folding rule with a sliding end for most pieces. I only unfold as much as I need not the whole thing. The measurement that you end up with is not important only that the measurement of each diagonal is the same or at least darn close.

If your carcase or drawer is out of square push it square now. Small items will usually stay put, but a large carcase may require extra support to hold it square. I find this very easy to do with go bars. Go bars are sticks just longer than the diagonals and about 3/4" square. When forced into the corners, they will force that particular diagonal longer and shorten the other. Don't make them too long or use too much force, as you can force apart the carcase you just spent so much time putting together.

Before the Glue Dries

The hammer and block mentioned earlier brings to mind something I saw while I was at school. Jim Krenov was gluing up something and working like a madman to get it done and I thought great, I am not the only one who semi-panics during a glue up. Then I thought, crap, he has been doing this for over 40 years and glue up is still a panic...

Fixed Shelves and Dividers

I use quite a bit of exposed joinery but I try to keep it subdued and make sure it fits in with the parts around it. Fixed shelves and dividers are a good example of this.

At each dado I fit a crosspiece with a through dovetail. This crosspiece, 2" wide

and as thick as the dado is wide, runs the full width of the cabinet and is notched to fit into the dado. Just make sure you remove enough material in this notch so the crosspiece does not spread the carcase. It should be a slip fit into the dado with no slack.

The remaining part, about 7/8", after the notch is removed, is cut into a dovetail. I cut this dovetail a little differently than dovetails used to hold corners together. I saw out a shoulder with a backsaw and pare the angle of the tail with a bench chisel. The part of the crosspiece that fits into the dado determines just where to cut the shoulder I cut the shoulder a bit less than an 1/8" deep, then carefully pare out a dovetail.

To cut the slot at the front of the dado for this tail, I put the cross piece into the carcase and mark directly from the tail with a sharp scratch awl. I use a marking gauge to set the depth of the cut and a square to mark the sides of the dovetail slot. Cut shy of the line with a backsaw. Remove the waste with a coping saw just above the depth line then pare to fit.

For a shelf or divider, I go ahead and glue in the crosspiece at this point. Prior to glue up though, make sure that the back edge of the crosspiece is planed straight and square for ease of gluing in the shelf/divider. After making up the shelf/divider, I slide it in from the back and glue it to the crosspiece. Both edges are planed straight and square, the front edge is glued to the crosspiece and the back edge of the shelf/divider is flush with the rabbet in the case sides. This way it can be glued to a rail or stile in the back panel. Gluing the back edge to the back panel adds considerable stiffness to a large carcase. You do not have to account for movement of the shelf/divider because the grain runs the same direction as the carcase sides.

Drawer Blades

Drawer blade is just a fancy name for a mortise and tenon frame that a drawer rides on. I think the name is of English origin, but I am not sure. Using this term helps avoid confusion with other parts of the cabinet. A drawer blade is made up of four parts, a front crosspiece, two runners, and a back crosspiece.

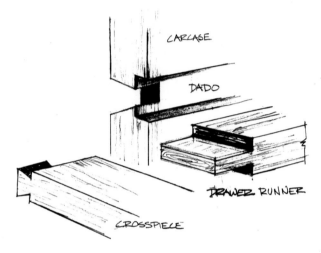

Fitting a drawer blade starts the same as a fixed shelf, but there is some extra joinery involved. After fitting the front crosspiece, you have to cut mortises into the back side prior to gluing it in. These mortises are for tenons on the runners that the drawers ride on. The runners slip into the dadoes, and then slide forward into the mortises. The back crosspiece has tenons that fit into mortises at the back of the runners. The crosspiece at the back keeps the runners tight in their dadoes in the case sides. I make this back crosspiece slightly thinner than the runners so it does not interfere with the drawers.

Make sure to leave a 3/8" gap between the back panel and the rear crosspiece to allow movement. It is important not to get any glue in the dado when gluing in the runners or the back crosspiece as the runners of the drawer blade run cross grain to the carcase side it is fitted to. The carcase will move, but the parts of the drawer blade won't.

Frame and Panel Backs

I always finish the back of my cabinets and about the only way I do this is with a frame and panel that is set flush with the sides of the carcase. Anyone who has done this knows it's difficult to obtain a joint with no visible glueline. (For detailed notes on how I make my frame and panels, see the Making Doors chapter)

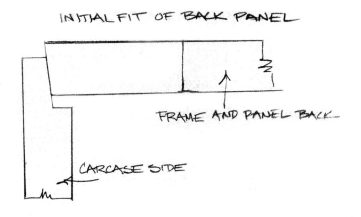

INITIAL FIT OF BACK PANEL

FRAME AND PANEL BACK

CARCASE SIDE

The reason it is difficult lies in the way most people fit a back panel, a square rabbet with a square edge panel. Done this way, you only have one good chance for a snug fit. There is a much better and easier way, simply put an angle on the rabbet in the carcase, then bevel the back panel to match. Putting an angle on the rabbet allows you to work up to a glue line free joint and also makes glue up a snap, with very little if any squeeze out.

Since you have already beveled the rabbet in the carcase, all you have to do now, is make the back panel slightly oversize. 1/8" to 3/16" should give you plenty of extra to bevel and trim during the fitting process.

Once the back panel is assembled and the glue is dry, remove the clamps and carefully bevel the edges of the panel to match the rabbet. For the first test fit, the panel should still be proud.

BEVELED RABBET

FRAME AND PANEL BACK

CARCASE SIDE

Remove the back panel and plane the edges carefully, while maintaining the bevel, until the panel goes all the way in. With patience and lots of test fits as you work, you should be able to achieve a joint with no visible glue line on all four sides.

Making the Cabinet Move

Whenever I make a cabinet, I always build to allow movement with the seasons. There is really no way to prevent seasonal movement of wood, even veneers will move. And just because I make room for the cabinet to move doesn't mean that this allowance has to show.

On most of my case pieces the carcase sets down into a separate dovetailed base frame and is rabbeted along the lower back edge to conceal movement. What this rabbet does is allow the carcase to expand over the top of the base frame. The base frame fits tight along the sides and front and the rabbet in the carcase provides 1/4" of room at the back for expansion.

This base is attached to the carcase with screws from underneath. These screws pass through strips that are glued to the inside face of the base frame. They are set into countersunk holes along the front edge and slotted holes with flat washers at the sides and back. I also fit glue blocks on the bottom side of the strips, between the screws, to add some strength. By fastening the base frame this way, all movement is focused at the back where it does not show.

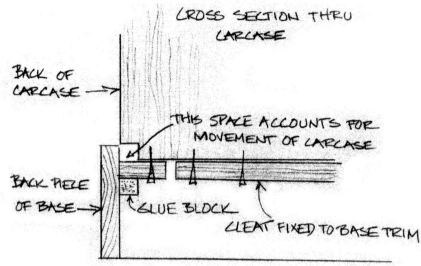

Fitting Trim

Trim is also attached to allow movement. I fix the side pieces to the carcase with a segmented sliding dovetail. The reason for the segments is the dovetails are attached to the carcase with screws at a cross grain location. By making the dovetails in segments even the concealed joinery is allowed to move.

Making a Segmented Sliding Dovetail

Plow a 3/8" x 3/8" groove on the backside of the trim. Use a Stanley 79 (a side rabbet plane) to angle the sides of the groove to create the female side of a sliding dovetail.

To make the male side, plane off the sides of a small stick to match the angle of the dovetail. It should be as long as the cabinet. When this stick slides evenly into the groove you are ready to mount it on the cabinet.

During the dry fit stage leave the stick in one piece. Mount it to the cabinet with #8 screws. I space the screws in line with the pins of the dovetails that hold the carcase together.

Slide the trim piece on to check the fit. There should be no gaps anywhere.

To tighten a loose fit, remove the strip and plane off a small amount of wood from the carcase side of the dovetail strip. If it's too tight, take a shaving or two from the angled side of the strip.

Pull it off and apply glue between every other pair of screws. The unglued sections will be removed after the glue sets up to create the segmented dovetails. To do this, cut through the dovetail with a backsaw at either side of each unglued section. Make sure you do not mark up the case side with the saw. It is best to cut a little short of the carcase and finish removing the waste with a sharp chisel and hammer.

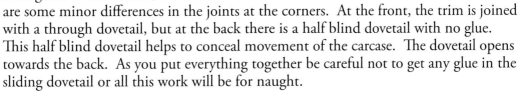

The front and back trim are both glued to the carcase, but there are some minor differences in the joints at the corners. At the front, the trim is joined with a through dovetail, but at the back there is a half blind dovetail with no glue. This half blind dovetail helps to conceal movement of the carcase. The dovetail opens towards the back. As you put everything together be careful not to get any glue in the sliding dovetail or all this work will be for naught.

Mortise and Tenon

Using slab side construction for the majority of my work, I don't use all that many mortise and tenons. When I do though there are two types I use, a through-wedged version for carcase pieces and the like and an open bridle version for frame and

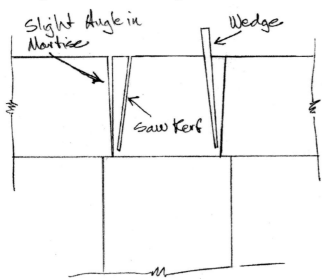

panels. A description of how I make the open bridle version is found in the Making Doors chapter and the following is how I make the other. I like using wedged tenons, as this joint does not rely completely on the glue to hold it together.

Marking Out

There are some things to consider when marking out all of the joinery. Think about the size of shoulders; mortise cheeks, thickness of tenons and

61

the dimensions of each individual member. By balancing all of these elements you make a stronger joint.

I wish there was a standard formula that applied to all mortise and tenons, but each situation has its own requirements. I tend to make my tenons just over 1/3 of the thickness of the piece it is cut on and size everything else in relation to this. This generally provides plenty of strength in both the mortise and tenon and provides for an adequate shoulder.

One other thing to consider is the size of your mortise chisels. You always want to match your joints to one of your chisels. Chopping out an odd size mortise is frustrating at best. Needless to say I have more mortise chisels than any other type and this gives me lots of latitude when laying out joinery.

Once I have the aforementioned worked out, I use a mortise gauge, square and sharp scratch awl to mark out for cutting. Make sure your awl is sharpened to a fairly fine point and use a light touch. I prefer an awl over a knife because the lines are more visible and they're easier to remove when you are finished with them.

Chopping the Mortise

I always cut the mortise first and fit the tenon to it. For small mortises, 5/16" wide or less, I just chop out the waste with a sash mortise chisel. For large mortises, I use a brace and bit to remove the bulk of the waste, and then clean out the rest with registered chisels.

To remove the waste with a mortise chisel, chop from end to end taking out a small chip with each mallet blow. Stop short of the ends to leave a small amount for clean up. You should be able to cut all the way into your mortise on the final cuts with your mortise chisel. I also clean up with a paring chisel if it needs it. I make them fairly smooth, but remember it's a glue joint not an exposed surface.

Cut a slight angle in the mortises to allow the tenon to expand as you tap in the wedges. This angle should only be about 1/16".

Cutting the Tenons

Saw out the shoulders of the tenons on a bench hook. Next, saw down to the shoulders to remove the cheek pieces of the tenons. Remember to cut short of your lines to leave a smidgen for final fitting to the mortises. I use a shoulder rabbet plane to clean up and fit the cheeks and shoulders of the tenon.

After the tenons fit their respective mortises saw an angled kerf in the tenon. This kerf should be cut at a right angle to the grain of the mortise piece. If it runs with the grain, you might split the mortise open when you tap the wedges in.

Start this kerf about 5/16" away from the edge of the tenon and it should stop about an 1/8" from the edge of the tenon at the shoulder. The angled kerf acts like a hinge when the wedge is driven home.

The wedges should taper from 1/8" down to nothing and only be as long as the kerf is deep. I make the wedges out of the same stock as the tenon, as the primary purpose of these wedges is mechanical and not for appearance sake.

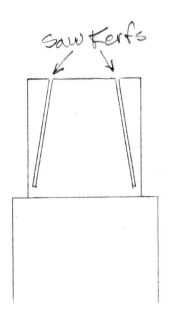

Gentle Curves from Patterns

One thing I found when I first started putting curves on my work was that it is very easy to get carried away with a curve. And for me it was (and still is for that matter) hard to see just the right curve unless I cut it out. Battens worked OK, but I still couldn't see the finished curve until I cut it out. Roughing out a curve with a pattern seemed to be the perfect solution.

Making patterns helps you decide on how much curve to put into a cabinet, base frame or edge of a table. They allow you to shape your curve and make any needed changes before you cut up expensive wood. It's easy to see the actual curve, and you end up with a durable pattern the next time you need a similar shape. One important thing to consider, at least for me, is to be subtle no matter what you are putting a curve on.

Cutting a Curve
There is not a good reason to torture yourself

while trying to find that perfect curve so use a clear, soft, easily shaped wood to make patterns. I have a small pile of clear, Western Red Cedar that I saved just for this purpose. Pine would also be a good choice, but stay away from knots.

Rough out a desired curve with a bow saw and finish up with planes and spokeshaves. I have found that when I am using a bow saw it is best to mark out my curve a little fat of where I want it to end up and cut right on my line for better control of the saw. This way cleaning up the edge will put the curve right where I want it.

What can really help you fair out a curve is to skew a block plane and run it almost sideways. This makes the plane act like a spokeshave because there is so little of the sole touching the stock.

When checking your progress, sight along the edge to find high and low spots and other irregularities. After that looks good, place the curve on a flat surface in front of an even light source, step back and eyeball the curve. This gives you an overall view of the curve and shows you if the curve is balanced from side to side. Trust your eyes to tell you when the curve is what boatbuilders call fair, no lumps or bumps. After you have done this only a few times it will be very easy to spot even the smallest of errors. You will have trained your eye in what to look for.

Coopered Panels

Putting a curve into a panel is not all that difficult. All you are really doing is beveling the joints during glue up to create an arch. When the glue is dry, the convex side of the panel is shaped with flat bench planes and the concave side is shaped with round bottom planes.

To make a panel with a gentle curve I just lightly bevel the edges then push all the pieces together to eyeball the curve. For panels that must be curved to a more exact line, I first make a guide pattern, and then bevel the parts to match the curve. Sometimes this pattern is only a line on cardboard and other times I make a re-usable pattern of soft wood. In certain instances this pattern can be used to help chop out the groove that the panel slips into.

For subtle curves you can clamp up in your regular clamps. Just use caution when tightening up or the panel will spring out of the clamps. Panels with a severe curve such as the ones I use in my corner cabinets require a different approach.

What I do is not any great innovation on my part; rather, I use a technique that has been around for centuries. It is called a "rubbed joint" and requires no clamps. There is no practical way to clamp up a severe curve, so a rubbed joint is the perfect

solution.

Rubbing the Joint

Joint the edges as usual. Apply glue to the piece that is still in the vise. Put the joint together and rub back and forth (about 1"). The joint will start to get stiff after a few minutes and you know it's time to stop "rubbing". Let the joint set up for about 20 or 30 minutes after which you can go on to the next joint. Simple, but very effective.

I use a pipe clamp vise to hold the pieces while I am planing and gluing. This vise is very easy to make up. You need two blocks with notches cut into them so they will hold the end of a pipe clamp in your face vise. Support the other end with a dowel that fits into a hole bored in the edge of your bench. Clamping the end of the pipe rather that the middle gives you more clearance by getting you away from the vise. The jaws of the clamp should face out, not up, for this to work. One thing to note is that a sliding 'T' handle pipe clamp works best in this situation. This pipe clamp "vise" allows me to continue working on a coopered panel even when the curve is quite severe.

Cleaning Up the Surfaces

To smooth the inside of a coopered panel, I have three round bottom planes that I made while I was at school. They each have a different radius for various curves. For the outside of the panel I just use my flat bench planes. These both leave a faceted surface that has a really

nice feel on the fingertips. You could take the time to remove all of these plane marks, but on coopered panels I prefer to leave them.

Broken Chamfers

When I was at school I think I drove my instructors crazy with my preference for chamfers over all other edge treatments. Well cut chamfers add a simple, yet pleasing detail to plain edges. My favorite technique is what I call broken chamfers. What this involves is chamfering all edges with a block plane or small spokeshave. A six-inch mill file works great on inside corners that are hard to get at with other tools. Then break the sharp edges by burnishing with a tenon offcut. This softens the edges without losing any definition.

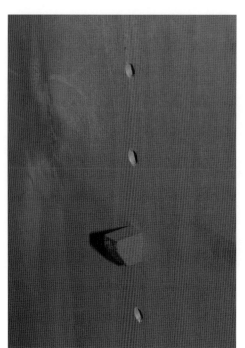

Working with files brings up an important point. If you insist on working with them without a handle, make sure to remove the tang. You won't put the tang through your hand, but you could give yourself one nasty cut if the file caught on something.

To remove the tang, score deeply around the base of it with a grinder, then place the file, tang up in a vise with the scored line just above the jaws of the vise. Wrap a rag around the tang and vise several times. Put on safety glasses, and then give the tang a quick smack with a hammer. The rag will prevent the tang from flying off as it breaks free and the safety glasses are there for "just in case". If the thought of this makes you the least bit nervous, take your file to a machine shop and ask them to cut off the tang with a cut off wheel not a torch. Grind down any sharp corners left and your file is now much safer to use.

Adjustable Shelves

Shelves are generally made of the same material as the case sides. This ensures that any movement is in tandem with the carcase. Shelves should just clear the sides of the carcase, with a fit that is neither too tight nor too loose.

One thing that I have found that adds a nice detail is to curve the lower edge of shelves. This is very easy to do with planes and spokeshaves. Just remove the lower front edge in a gentle arching curve with a scrub plane and clean up with a block plane and spokeshave.

Shelf Pins

I keep things pretty simple when it comes to shelf supports. I use 1" pieces of 3/16" brass rod or frequently I will make small wood supports like the ones in the picture. I mark out the holes for shelf supports by making a pattern stick. This stick is used to mark each vertical row of shelf holes. By using the same stick at each location, all the holes end up on the level. I only drill a few holes, usually four, for each shelf as there is no reason to run the holes top to bottom as the shelves rarely move much beyond their intended location.

When drilling all these holes a masking tape flag on the bit is a good depth indicator. It not only tells you visually when to stop drilling but also if you are working on a horizontal surface the tape will sweep the surface when you reach the proper depth. I use long mask painters' tape (the expensive blue stuff), as it is easier to remove from a drill bit when I am done with it.

To keep the shelves from sliding forward, cut a shallow notch in the bottom of the shelf at the location of each shelf pin. This not only prevents the shelf from sliding forward but also conceals the pins from sight.

Housed Sliding Dovetail

Large pieces of furniture reach a point where it is no longer practical to leave them in one piece. They take up too much space in your shop and are next to impossible to move around, not only in your shop, but also by whoever ends up with the piece. This last dilemma lead me to come up with a knock-down design after a client who had requested a china cabinet was facing a possible move to Norway and needed the piece to come apart for shipping.

There are endless ways to connect two case pieces, but most of the techniques I have seen are lacking in one way or another.

I came up with

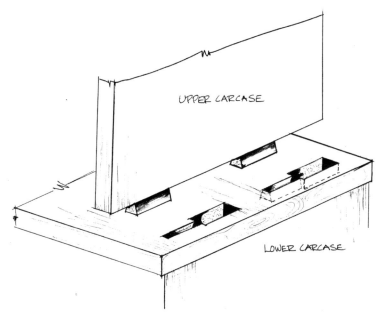

a straightforward and strong connection using a housed sliding dovetail. The finished joint is easy to assemble and take apart, uses no hardware and does not show front or back when assembled. Another plus to this method is that it takes very few tools and is easy to work up a practice piece to make sure you understand what's going on with the joinery.

Making the Upper Carcase

The lower carcase needs to be finished before you start on the upper case. I make the upper case about 1" narrower than the lower case. This moves the dovetails away from the edge of the lower carcase adding some needed strength in the dovetail

slots.

Before gluing up the upper carcase, I cut the dovetail on the case sides with a dovetail plane. If you do not have a dovetail plane, chisels and a cutting gauge would also work. When finished the dovetail should be 1/8" narrower than the case side and approximately 1/2" to 5/8" long depending on the thickness of the lower carcase top.

Next, I complete all the joinery on the upper case leaving the dovetails extending below the bottom of the carcase. The back panel should be flush with the shoulder of the dovetails.

After the glue dries, I cut down the dovetails into two small ones on each side. Placement of these is critical. The dovetails must be far enough forward to ensure that the escapements don't show when the upper carcase is installed, and far enough apart so they do not interfere with each other.

Marking Out

At this point, I place the completed upper carcase onto the lower carcase and mark the front, back and sides of each dovetail, and then use these reference lines to mark out the escapements and dovetails.

Escapements

Once it is all marked out, I remove the bulk of the waste from the escapements with a brace and bit, then pare to the lines with a chisel. The upper case should just fit the escapements with no extra room.

Cutting the Dovetail Slots

The hard part here is that you are working blind; you can't see what you are working on. Fitting the first 1/4" or so of each dovetail makes a good reference to fit the remainder. There is a lot of test fitting, but I work slowly, paring carefully up to my marked lines. Also, I am not trying to get the fit all at one go; rather I am going a bit at a time. The goal is a snug joint that goes together with hand pressure, a little looser than a glue joint, but tighter than a well fit drawer.

Finishing Up

Once the upper carcase slides all the way forward, you need to pull it off and apply a good coat of paste wax to all parts of the dovetails. The wax helps the two parts of the joint work like they are supposed to. You now have a simple, clean and elegant connection for a two-piece cabinet.

Making Doors

There are numerous ways to put a door together, but after trying many of them I have settled on one way to make most of my doors and frame and panels. The joint I use on my doors and frames is called a partial miter, open bridle mortise and tenon. It may have some other name, but I have not seen one for it. The open bridle joinery is easily and efficiently cut with hand tools and the mitered part comes from an old molding joint. The miter saves the hassle of stop-cutting a rabbet or a groove in the frame member and allows you to mold the inner edge with a molding plane without messing up any joinery. While I skip this last step of molding the edge, I do have a preference for this joint.

The best reason I have for using this joint has to be how it changes the appearance of a door or frame and panel. The small miter on the inside corner "softens" the joinery and draws your eye away from all the straight lines of the door.

Cutting Stock to Size

First of all, I rip, crosscut and plane the stock to size. Frame pieces are about 3/4" thick; stiles 1 3/4" to 2" wide with the top rail 1/8" narrower and the bottom rail 1/8" wider (Frame pieces for a back panel assembly are considerably larger in width). I determine lengths of frame pieces by measuring the height and widths of the opening they are going into then add 1/8". This extra length is cleaned off after glue up and

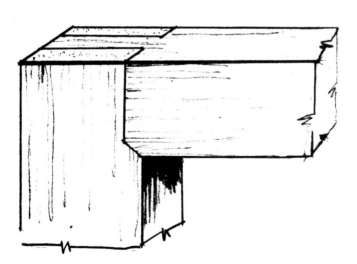

during the fitting process. I determine which is the face side and which is the groove or rabbet side, then I can mark out the joints for cutting.

Marking Out

I clamp two frame pieces, either the rails or stiles, together with a small C-clamp to save a bit of time while marking out. This way I can mark two ends at once. Rather than measuring out each joint, mark this baseline onto your stiles directly from the rails, and vice versa. This helps to ensure the squareness of the finished frame and may also help you avoid a layout error by eliminating measurements.

How Much Miter
Next, I determine how much of the frame will be mitered. The mitered portion of the frame is determined by how deep your groove or rabbet is. This dimension should be slightly deeper than the groove.

JOINERY LINE
(SCRIBED)

MITER

WIDTH OF MITER

THIS SECTION REMOVED

BASELINE (PENCIL)

Typically, a 1/4" deep panel groove will require a 5/16" miter. For a rabbeted frame, the mitered portion matches the depth of the rabbet.

Once you have determined the size of the mitered portion of the frame, scribe a line on the groove side of the frame piece, this distance from the pencil line. I call this the joinery line, as it is the base of the mortise and tenons. No cutting, with the exception of the miters a little later, will take place beyond this line, so you need to carry it all the way around your stock with a square and scratch awl. Remember to use a light touch with the scratch awl, as you do need to eventually remove these lines.

Using a Mortise Gauge
Marking out the lines for the mortise and tenons comes next. Using the chisel you are going to remove the waste with, set the movable points of a mortise gauge, typically 5/16" on a 3/4" thick frame. Set the fence of the gauge to center the points on the stock. The easy way to do this is by pressing the points into the stock, flip the gauge to the other side and make another mark with the points, if you have set the fence correctly the points will be right on one another, it not split the difference and try again.

Never mark beyond your joinery line and always use the face side of the piece you are marking as the reference for the gauge.

Cutting the Mortise
I use a hand brace, backsaw and a mortise chisel to cut the mortises. I bore through with the brace and bit just above the base of the mortise. The bit I use is just a tad smaller than the mortise. Then I cut to the waste side of my lines with the backsaw. Most of the waste will usually drop right out when I get to the bottom of the joint.

72

One thing I started doing recently with my backsaw is to cut against the grain. This means tipping the stock towards you rather than away as you normally would. It helps your backsaw, which has crosscut teeth, cut more efficiently in the ripping mode which is what it's doing cutting a tenon or mortise. You could also re-cut the teeth on your saw into rip teeth, but then your saw is useless for cross cutting and I don't want to maintain two saws when one will suffice.

Next, I chop out the small amount of waste remaining with a mortise chisel and clean up the sides of the mortises, if needed, with a paring chisel.

Cutting the Tenons

I use a back saw to cut the tenons, the same saw to cut both the shoulders and the cheeks. On the cheeks, I cut against the grain, as mentioned above, after the shoulders are cut on a bench hook. Next, I use a shoulder rabbet plane to clean up the tenons until they fit the mortises. Don't mess with the shoulders of the joint at this point.

Marking the Miters

Now I mark the miters and the portion of the frame to be removed that allows the miters to come together. I use a pencil to mark the miters (45 degrees) from the penciled baseline to the joinery line on the face and back of my stock. I use a small sliding T-bevel to do this. For a rabbeted frame you only have to mark the face side.

I set a marking gauge equal to the mitered portion of the frame and mark the portion of the frame to be removed, on both sides for a paneled frame and only on the front for a rabbeted frame. This scribed line should start where the point of the gauge intersects the marked miter (at the joinery line) and stop at the end grain of the frame piece.

Cutting the Miters

I cut off this marked section of wood on the tenon piece down to the tenon shoulder, but leave the extra on the mortise piece for now. I plow the panel groove 1/4" deep and 5/16" wide or cut my rabbet on the back side at this point. After I have plowed the groove, I cut off the extra wood on the mortise piece. The reason I leave the extra on the mortise piece is that the depth stop of my plow plane, a Stanley 45, needs this for a reference. On the tenon piece the extra wood is just in the way.

Next, I pare the shoulders of the mortise piece to the marked line(s). Make sure to be extra careful to maintain squareness when removing this waste. It is very important to the final fit of the joint.

I rough out the miters next, on both the tenon and the mortise piece with a backsaw and a chisel but leave the line for final fitting.

Fitting the Joint

Final paring of the miter on the mortise pieces comes next. I do this freehand due to its small size, but you could use a miter block. A miter block is just a piece of wood that clamps onto your stock to guide a chisel.

I clean up the shoulder of the tenons at this point with a shoulder rabbet plane and after I am pleased with the fit I pare the miter carefully to fit against the miter on the mortise piece. With a bit of careful paring the miters and the mortise and tenons should all close up together. But do not fret if things are not as they should be as it is easy to make adjustments.

Making Adjustments

All corrections to an ill fitting joint should be made to the tenon piece. For the simple reason that corrections are harder to make on the mortise piece. Loose miters are easily fixed by trimming back the shoulders of the tenon. Shoulders and tenons that don't quite close up just need a bit of trimming on the miters.

Make sure to keep things square and don't forget to keep an eye on the tenon in the mortise as well because everything has to close up at the same time. And don't worry, like most things, it's easier to do than write about.

Work slowly with sharp tools and everything will be right on the money. Making corrections does have a price.

Heavy corrections will make the door smaller than planned and could also put it out of square. This is my reason for making doors and frames oversize. I always have an allowance for fitting and corrections.

Making Panels

I keep my panels pretty simple. Generally, panels are 3/8" thick and I just rabbet the edges to fit the groove in the frame. I chamfer all corners and edges of the panel and I place the flat side out.

Sizing and Fitting Panels

I have a pretty easy way to size panels. Like everyone, I have a lot of narrow, thin scraps lying around and I put them to good use by cutting one of them to fit into the groove of a dry assembled door or frame. This eliminates measurements and by cutting the piece that sets the width a bit short you can account for room needed for seasonal movement of the panel. I tend to leave a gap between the panel and the frame of about 3/16" for seasonal changes and for ease of assembly I usually leave a bit of room in the length of a panel.

When cutting the rabbets that thin down the edges of the panels I use a Mullet block to gauge the thickness of the remaining wood. A Mullet block is just a small piece of wood with grooves plowed in it that match the cutters in my plow plane. This way I don't have to keep measuring to get the thickness right. Once the panel slides evenly in the appropriate groove in the Mullet block I can stop planing the edge. I know that the panel will fit the frame it is going into.

Glue Up

Glue up is simple. After dry clamping to check the fits, take things apart and butter the joints with glue. Pull everything together with pipe clamps, then C-clamp (5" clamps for pressure) the corners with blocks the same size as the joint to spread the clamping pressure. At this point I remove the pipe clamps, but I like to leave the

C-clamps overnight.

Check for squareness by measuring the diagonals with a folding rule or a stick made for this purpose. I am not concerned about the measurement only that the diagonals are the same length. Usually out of square is not a problem, as the joinery tends to collect itself during clamp up. If there is a slight misalignment pushing together the corners of the larger of the diagonals will usually correct the problem.

In Conclusion

You can see from looking at the finished joint, as your eye moves up or across the frame members, when you get to the corner, the joinery forces you to shift what you are looking at. To my eye this "soft" corner is much more appealing to look at than the typical square corner joinery.

Arch Top Doors

Like a lot of people, I shied away from putting curves on my work for a long time. I thought they would be too much work and generally not worth the effort, but I finally dove in and put some gentle curves on one of my cabinets. I found that placing a gentle curve along the tops of doors softens the rectilinear lines I am partial to and added a lot to my work.

Curve the Cabinet First

Start by making a cabinet with an arch in the door opening. The arch should be no more than 5/16" over 30", 3/8" or so in larger cabinets. My goal is a subtle arch that's flatter in the center and gets tighter at the ends. You could use a much more exaggerated curve and this technique will still work, I just prefer mild curves. For a simple way to get a clean curve see the Carcase Joinery chapter about making curves from patterns.

There is one major difference in the construction of arch top doors compared to simple square doors. In a cabinet with two doors with an arch, the center stiles are longer than the hinge side stiles and a curved rail connects them. While this could get confusing, I have a simple way to lay out and cut the joinery. Just what joinery you use is not critical, but I use the same open bridle mortise and tenon for all my doors.

Cutting Out Stock

When making the frame pieces, leave the stiles about 1/4" too long and cut the bottom rails to length + 1/8". The top rail is where you account for the differences in the length of the stiles. While the top rails are also left 1/8" long they have to be wider than the finished size by the amount of arch as well. For example, 2" frame + 5/16" arch = 2 5/16" rough size for the curved rail.

With some careful selection of wood you should be able to find some grain that follows your curve. If you don't have curved grain, use quarter sawn stock. Flat sawn stock might stand out too much.

Marking Out

To make things easier, all joinery is left square and length measurements for the rails and stiles are mostly eliminated by using the cabinet to directly mark the parts.

First mark the centerline of the opening, both top and bottom. Place the stiles into the cabinet, just behind the arch, at the appropriate location for each and mark the curve directly onto them, but don't cut them off at this point. This curved line is your reference for laying out the joinery. Carry the marked curve onto the inside edge of each stile with a square and mark out the joint from this line.

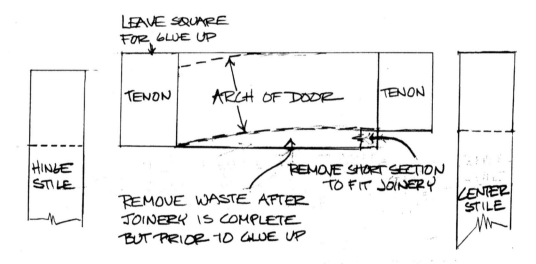

Cutting the Joints

Even though I use the same joinery for square doors, with arch top doors there is an additional step involved. Before marking out the joinery on the rails, I remove a short section of the lower edge, cutting 3/4" or so beyond the tenon shoulder. It is removed only from the end of the top rail that is attached to the center stile. The amount I remove is equal to the amount of curve I put into the cabinet.

Removing this short section accounts for the difference in length between the hinge and center stiles and allows me to fit all the joinery without the curve getting in the way. After I have removed this section of the rail, I mark out and finish fitting all the joinery.

Once the joinery fits, but prior to glue up, I shape the curve on the inside edge of the top rail with a spokeshave. To make sure that it matches the curve on the cabinet, I just place the curve pattern that determined the arch in the cabinet onto the rail at the appropriate location to mark it. Leave the outer part of the top rail square until after glue up.

Cutting a rabbet for glass or a groove for a panel is usually not a problem, as the curves I use are very subtle, and in the short length of the rail, the edge you are working with actually has very little curve. Grooves are plowed with a Stanley 45 and

rabbets are cut with a rabbet plane. I don't worry about the base of the groove being curved as it does not show, but sometimes I do have to curve a rabbet and this is easily done with a bullnose rabbet plane.

One thing to consider if you are working with glass is the ability of your glass supplier to cut curves. Most of the time curved glass must be special ordered. Glass cut on an angle (i.e. not square) works just fine with the subtle curves I use and the way that I mount glass in a door. The following section of this chapter goes over how I mount glass in more detail. After your rabbet or groove is cut, you are ready to glue things together.

Glue Up and Fitting

During glue up you can see why you leave the top rail square. It provides a square surface to clamp up. The hardest part of gluing up a door with a curve is determining if the door is square or not. The method I use most often is to measure the diagonals; if they match everything is square. But on a door with a curved rail you can no longer trust the diagonals because one stile is longer than the other. So instead of measuring the diagonals, I just place a try square on the inside edge of the bottom rail to check for square. There are no clamps to get in your way at this location.

Shaping and Fitting the Door

After glue up, I first fit the hinge and bottom side of the door to the cabinet. Then I place my door into the cabinet, just behind the arch of the opening, to mark the curve directly onto the upper edge of the door. By marking the curve this way, you ensure the doors are a perfect match to the arched opening.

After using a bow saw to cut the curve, I use spokeshaves and planes to shape the door to the cabinet. I always leave things a bit snug until I have a final fit for the hinges.

Don't be too concerned about repeatedly removing and installing doors. If you want that just right fit you will have to do so. I always aim to get a fit with a gap equal to a business card on the top, bottom and hinge side and a gap of 2 or 3 cards where two doors come together or one door meets the side of a cabinet. For more on fitting doors look to the end of this chapter.

Doors with Glass

Whenever I make doors with glass, the glass is always set in relatively deep rabbets in the frame, and held in place with beveled strips of wood on the back side of the door. The strips are fastened to the shoulder of the rabbet with brass escutcheon pins. Should the glass need to be replaced, the strips easily pop off and can be reused.

Holding glass in this way is nothing new. It's an old technique that works because it's simple and practical, and it looks good whether the door is open or closed.

With glass front cabinets, the focus is not on the furniture, but what's inside it. Before you begin making the cabinet, think about how a glass front will affect the design and construction. Everything is now visible, so the layout and fit of the joints on the inside of the cabinet are as important as those on the outside.

Choosing Wood and Glass

Standard window glass is only 3/32" thick. I buy it cut to order at a local glass shop. When safety is a factor (when the glass will be near the floor in a household with children, for example), I use tempered glass.

Glass weighs about three times as much as wood. But the weight of a simple door glazed with 3/32" glass is roughly the same as that of a similar wood panel door.

Glass has a slight green tinge. The effect is more noticeable as the thickness of the glass increases, and it can alter the color of the wood behind it. Sometimes the effect can be pleasing, and sometimes not. Test it by looking at wood samples through the glass you intend to use.

Making Door Frames

When sizing the cabinet door-frames, keep in mind that the clear front affects the apparent widths of the frame pieces. The same size frame you'd use for a wood panel can look too heavy with glass. When I make a typical cabinet door, the frame pieces are about 5/8" to 3/4" thick, depending on the thickness of the glass. I make the rails and stiles about 1 3/4" wide with the top rail 1/8" narrower. The rabbet depth is two-thirds the thickness of the frame. The joinery I use on my doors is described in the first part of this chapter so there isn't much sense in going over it again.

Installing the Glass

When the doors are made, but not finished, I take them to the glass shop to have the glass cut. Sometimes though I only take measurements or make patterns and this has worked as well. A good slip fit is desirable for the glass, if it's loose in the frame, it may rattle when you open and close the door. There's no need to allow for movement in either the wood or the glass.

If the glass is too snug in the frame, adjust the fit with a rabbet plane. If the glass is a little small, you can shim out the rabbets with thin slivers of wood. Nothing will show once the beveled strips are in place.

Fitting the Strips

The beveled strips are sized so that when they're installed, they will stand slightly proud of the frame and are a little narrower than the rabbet. The strips are not rectangular in section, they bevel about 5 to 8 degrees. This makes them less visible from the outside.

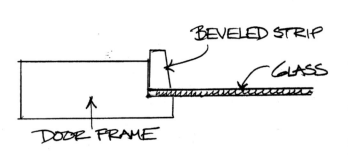

I rip the strips from long scraps of the same wood as the frame. I plane all four sides on a small vise mounted bench I built for handling small pieces. It has a small stop made from a brass screw (brass because it will cause less damage to an errant plane iron than steel) and a light fence tacked on to hold the strips for planing. Then I lightly chamfer all the edges with a small spokeshave.

When the finish on the door is dry, set the glass in the rabbet, and fit the strips. First, fit the top and bottom and then the sides. I cut them a little long with a backsaw and then pare them to fit with a chisel. Because of the bevel the side pieces are cut at a slight angle. The best way to fit them is by paring away a little at a time. Once the strips are fitted, I lightly file the ends to match the chamfers on the edges.

Fastening the Strips

I use #18 escutcheon pins, 5/8" long to hold the strips in place. I like the look of the brass head, and the pins make a secure fastening.

With the strips fitted in place, I mark the locations for the escutcheon pins every 4" or 5". I remove the strips and drill the shank holes for a push fit. Use a #53 or #54 drill, depending on the wood. Check the fit in a piece of scrap to be sure. I drill the holes at right angles to the bevel and clean up both sides of the hole by turning a small countersink, a few times by hand.

I put the escutcheon pins partway in the shank holes in the strips and put the strips back in place on the glass. Holding the strip firmly in place, I lightly tap each pin to mark the frame for the pilot holes. After removing the strips and the glass, I use the marks in the frame as centers for drilling the pilot holes. I use a #55 drill for a hammer fit, and I drill at about 5 degrees off the perpendicular, the amount of the bevel.

Everything is ready for final assembly, but first I finish both the strips and the inside of the door with paste wax.

Final Assembly

Before installing the glass, I clean it one last time. I put it back in the frame, put the strips in place and protect the glass with a piece of cardboard cut from a cereal box. I set the escutcheon pins with a 3 oz Warrington hammer. It's light and narrow, perfect for such work. Don't try to drive the pins in one blow-take it slowly. Be careful not to hit the strips, or they will be marred by the hammer.

If an escutcheon pin goes into the frame too easily because the diameter of the pilot hole is a little too big or too deep, you can tighten it up by bending the pin. Just hit it with the narrow end of a Warrington hammer to put in a slight curve. When you put the pin back in the pilot hole, it'll snug up nicely.

Fitting Doors

Once you are done with a door you need to mount it on the cabinet. I find the easiest way to do this is by first fitting the bottom edge, and then plane the hinge side to fit flush against the carcase. Fit the top edge and finally the handle side last. At this stage, leave the door snug in the opening; final fitting comes after you have mounted the hinges.

Next, I mortise in the hinges on the door. The hinges are lined up with the inner edge of the rails. I only put one screw into each hinge, in case I need to make adjustments. By offsetting the remaining pilot holes you can move a hinge in or out on the door, that is if you didn't go ahead and drill all the holes first.

Gaps and Setbacks of Doors

One thing to consider at this point is how much gap you want around the doors. I never trust my hinges to set this dimension. They usually have too much space between the leaves and this creates too large of a gap for my taste. I always try to get a very small gap on the hinge side of a door, equal to the thickness of a business card. If needed, just set the hinges slightly deeper in their mortises to compensate.

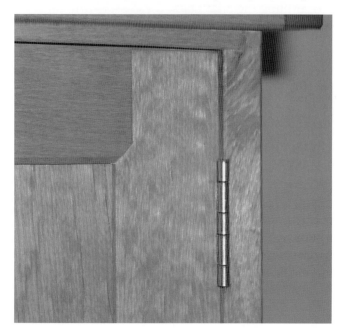

Once the hinges are on the door, set the door into the opening and mark the mortise locations on the carcase. Whenever I mount doors into a carcase, I always set them back by about 1/16". This is more pleasing to the eye than setting them flush with the carcase, and it can help disguise minor variations between the door, the cabinet and your mounting of the hinges. Once again, use only one screw at each hinge for now.

Final Fitting

If you were careful in your mounting of the hinges and the planing of the door, it should open and close, but still be snug. Plane off the tight spots, and try to leave a space equal to the gap on the hinge side along the top and bottom and 2 or 3 business cards along the carcase or door it butts up against. And, yes, you will be taking the door on and off numerous times to get the right fit.

Once you have the fit you are after, go ahead and drill pilot holes and install the rest of your screws. Be sure to check the fit again, as fastening all the screws can sometimes mess with your fit.

Fixing Problems

Everyone who has ever made and mounted a door has sometimes run into the problem of a door that does not fit right, either the door or the carcase is not flat. There is a way to fix this, or at least to conceal it from sight. If found early enough, you can taper the stile on the hinge side of the door. This taper, depending on which end it is on, will bring the handle side of the door in line with the carcase or door it butts up against. If you still need some adjustment, taper the handle side to fit prior to mounting the handle.

Risers

I install a small riser in each door opening to support the doors when closed. Risers are pieces of wood, 1/4" x 1/4" x 3/8"L mortised into the cabinet bottom on the catch side. The block goes in end grain up and leave about 1/16" sticking out. After the glue dries it's filed down until its height equals the gap between the carcase and the door. When the riser is filed down to the correct height, carefully chamfer the exposed edges with a chisel. The door rests lightly on the riser and opens and closes easily.

Door Stops

I first learned about pressure bars to hold doors closed and act as stops while I was at school. Pressure bars give a nice feel to an opening and closing door as there is no click or grab, just a slight tension, that is more than enough to hold the door closed. Pressure bars are very simple to install above a door and are made of only three parts; a screw, a spring and a small block of wood.

A pressure bar pivots on the screw and uses the spring to apply pressure to hold down the door against the riser. A rabbet cut into the bar acts as a stop. The shape of the bar is not all that critical. Leave enough wood to cut the stop into the bar and to drill a small hole for the screw and spring.

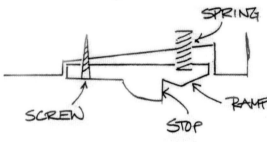

Making the Bar

I start with a small block, about 3/8" square by 1 1/2"L. Next I divide it up into thirds. At the back I thin it down to 1/8". The center third or stop portion is left full thickness and at the front section I thin it down to 3/16" and file off the leading edge to shape a small ramp that the door rides against as it closes. The ramp only goes back 1/4", and just behind this ramp I relieve some of the thickness to create a ridge that pushes down on the door when the bar is installed. Drill a shallow hole on the underside of the ramp to hold a small spring and drill and countersink a hole in the back section for a #2 screw.

I don't mess with the stop portion until after the mortise is cut.

Cutting the Mortise

I close the door and mark the inside edge onto the cabinet. To locate and size the mortise, I place the pressure bar about an inch away from the handle side of the door. The leading edge of the stop portion is just outside the line I marked for the inner edge of the door in the closed position. Next, I scribe around the bar and this scribed line is my mark to cut the mortise.

The bar should slide in and out of the mortise easily. By the screw pivot it should be the same depth as the bar is thick, but at the front there should be room for the bar to move into the mortise as the door closes. Drill a shallow hole at the front of the mortise to hold the spring. This hole should line up with the spring hole in the pressure bar.

After the mortise is cut, I place the bar into the mortise without the screw or spring and close the door. Because the stop portion of the bar was located proud of the line of the inside edge of the door, all I have to do to get just the fit I want is to slowly pare away the stop portion until the door closes all the way.

Mounting the Bar

Once I have the fit of the door I want, I fasten the bar into the mortise with a #2 screw. The hole through the bar should be slightly reamed out to allow the bar to pivot on the screw. Adjust feel of the door by clipping the spring shorter or by deepening the spring hole in the mortise.

Door Pulls

I always seem to leave pulls until last. Maybe it's because I haven't decided what I am going to use until now. One way to make interesting and original door pulls

quickly, and with little sweat, is to buy commercially available knobs and modify them.

I take very ordinary round wooden knobs and use a rasp to knock off the sides to create an oval shape. Then I file around the base to make a simple bevel. I clean these up with files and sandpaper. Sometimes I shorten the tenon and use a screw from the inside for extra strength.

Drawers

There are a myriad of ways to make drawers. But generally, I use only one way to make drawers. The sides are tapered on the inner face, but the outside stays square. This type of construction might be attributed to the Shakers. The Shaker's were making drawers this way over 100 years ago. I think the main reason this type of drawer never caught on is because it is not very friendly to machine methods.

There are some good reasons for using tapered drawer sides, such as the increased wear resistance of the wider bottom edge, a more pleasing narrow upper edge when the drawer is open, a thicker cross section where the groove for the bottom panel is plowed and they save time and labor during construction. Making drawers with tapered sides is no harder and requires no more work than straight side drawers. About the only difference is that during construction you have to do some careful layout.

There is one other thing that also stands out about my drawers, the smoothness of their operation. Many people are surprised to find nothing but wood to wood contact between the drawer and cabinet. The ease at which they open and close is achieved with careful attention to fit, both during construction and with the final fit to the drawer pocket.

Making the Parts Fit

A well fitting drawer is easy to achieve when all of the parts of a drawer are pre-fit to the opening it's going into. And it is absolutely essential when making drawers that slide with wood on wood. This does not mean cutting the parts to a cut list, but actually using the opening to size the parts. Work to fit, not measurements.

Most of the time I use 3/4" stock for the fronts and sides of my drawers and 1/2"stock for the back. Small drawers

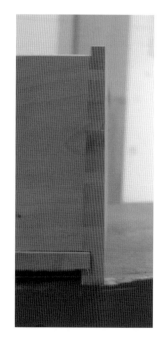

use slightly thinner material. The length of the back piece should just fit the opening and it should be a little over an inch shorter than the opening is tall. Trim the side pieces to the proper height, 1/8" clearance is sufficient for 5" or 6" drawers. Make adjustments for shorter or taller drawers. Next, I cut them to length, generally 5/8" shorter than the drawer pocket. The sides need to be this much shorter than the opening to account for the joinery and to allow for movement of the carcase sides. Drawer fronts are cut to the same height as the sides, but should only just start into the openings.

By cutting all of the parts this way, you have far less to do during the final fit of the drawer and results in a better fitting drawer.

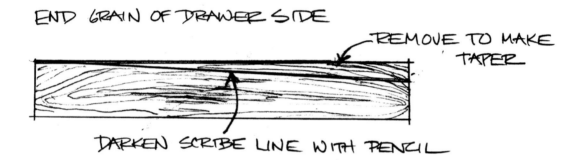

Marking Out the Tapers

Once all the parts are fitted, I mark the sides either R or L at the outside top edge. Fronts and backs are marked for easy identification later.

To lay out the taper on a drawer side use a marking gauge set to 1/2", scribe a line down the top surface of each side. Make sure to use the outer face of the drawer side as a reference for the fence of the marking gauge. Using the scribed line on the top edge and the bottom inside corner of the drawer side as a reference points for a straight edge, scribe a line on the end grain between these two points. This sets the angle of the taper. Make sure to mark both ends of each drawer side. Don't bother with an adjustable bevel, as it's more hassle than it's worth

Plane the Tapers

I use a scrub plane to cut the tapers. It's quick and easy to knock off the waste with a scrub plane then clean it up with a jointer plane. I find that darkening the tapered scribe line with a pencil is very helpful when doing this. It makes your line much easier to see on the endgrain.

Plowing the Bottom Panel Groove

Prior to cutting the dovetails I plow a groove for the drawer bottom. This helps you lay out the dovetails by ensuring the groove exits in a tail and not in a pin or between them. You want the groove to come out of a tail so that it does not show on a finished drawer.

Placement of the groove is also important to ensure there is clearance below the bottom panel to install a drawer stop. For the 1/2" bottom panels I use on an average size drawer, the top of the groove is placed 1" from the bottom of the drawer resulting in 1/2" clearance for a stop. When plowing the groove make sure it is parallel to the square outside of the drawer, not the tapered inner face.

Keeping All the Pieces in Order

I have a simple way to do this. I lay all the parts out and number the corresponding corners in the groove for the bottom panel. This way the marks don't show later nor do you have to remove them. For the back piece I mark the lower edge where the bottom panel will conceal it. This also helps with glue up, as there is no guessing which part goes where during the heat of the moment.

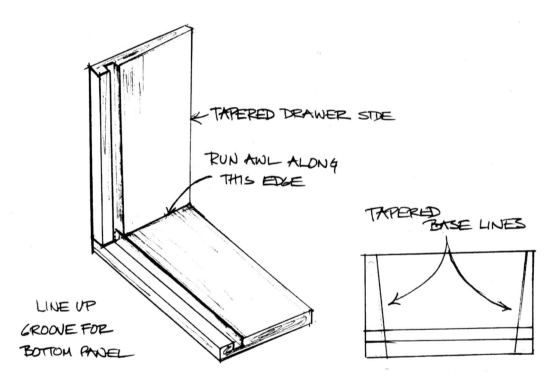

Marking Out the Dovetails

Before I cut the tails, I use the side pieces to mark the tapered baselines on the front and back pieces. I lay the front on the bench with the top edge facing away from me, the outer face of the board downward. Take the appropriate side piece and stand it up on the inside of the drawer face, align the groove for the drawer bottom and make sure the outer face is flush with the end grain of the front, then scribe the taper.

For the back piece line up the marked bottom edge with the top of the groove in the side piece and, once again, make sure the outer face of the side is flush with the end grain of the back piece.

When marking the back piece, carry the scribe line around to the face side with a square and straight edge. On the drawer front, instead of carrying the taper to the face side, you mark the endgrain with the same marking gauge you used to scribe the length of the tails on the drawer sides. The fronts are attached with half blind dovetails, so there is no need to scribe the taper on the face.

Cutting the Dovetails

Now is the time to layout all your dovetails. I no longer make any more scribe lines than I find necessary. If you are more comfortable with scribe lines, by all means use them, I am just used to working with very few of them. I cut dovetails by eye and with practice you will find that this is not very difficult. This is one place I differ from dovetails on larger work, as I do not use dividers to set spacing of the tails on drawer parts or other small pieces.

After you have marked all your drawer parts, it's time to put them into a vise for cutting. The flat front and back are not a problem, but for the tapered sides you need to make some adjustments. Take two tapered sides and clamp them into the vise at the same time. This forms a rectangle that your vise will easily hold. Remember when you are putting these parts into your vise you must stagger them so you cut the tails in only one piece at a time. What you need to ensure is that saw cuts are square to the outside face of the drawer side, not the tapered inner face.

After you have gotten to this point, cutting the dovetails is pretty straightforward. Just make sure you follow the tapered scribe lines. Since I have already gone over how I cut dovetails in another chapter I don't think it is necessary to repeat myself. What I have included here are things that differ from regular dovetails. For more on dovetails just refer back to the dovetail section in the Carcase Joinery chapter.

Final Fitting

Pre-fitting the parts allows me to take only a few passes with a plane after glue up to get a piston fit. To make planing easier, I fit the drawer to it's opening prior to fitting the bottom panel. I use what is called a drawer board. This is just a board that hangs off the bench and allows you to plane any side of the drawer without placing it into a vise. Not having the bottom panel installed is the key to making a drawer board work. By using a drawer board instead of a vise you will save a lot of time as you move between the carcase and your bench.

Bottom Panel

I keep things simple and use a 1/2" thick panel in the bottom of my drawers. I use Western Red Cedar most of the time because it has a nice subtle scent and when I want something with a stronger scent I use Eastern Red Cedar. The panel floats in the groove and is attached at the back with a screw. The screw fits in a slot to account for movement. And, no, I never glue in the bottom panel.

Drawer Stops

Drawer stops serve two purposes in my cabinets. They stop the drawer from hitting the back of the drawer pocket and they also determine the setback of the drawer front. I use a setback of about 1/16".

To fit the stops, the bottom panel is still out of the drawer. I use two stops per drawer, fastened to the crosspiece just behind the drawer front. These stops just clear the bottom panel of the drawer when it's installed and are about 2" long, 3/4" wide and 3/8" thick.

The easy way to fit these is to place the drawer into the pocket. Apply glue to two of your stops and place them on the crosspiece through a partially open drawer. Hold them down from below or above and close the drawer until the drawer front has the proper setback. After the glue starts to set up, about 2 minutes, open the drawer and apply a C-clamp to keep it in place while the glue dries. Be careful not to shift the stop as you tighten up the clamp. If you feel the need you could add a screw later for extra strength.

Drawer Pulls

The most important thing about pulls on drawers is consistent placement. Drawers are usually stacked and any error in placement stands out like a sore thumb. Straight edges and plumb lines are an immense help when laying out pulls.

I always match the pulls between drawers and doors when both are used on the same piece

of furniture. The Making Doors chapter goes over a good way to make pulls. Another thing to keep in mind is to make pulls that are in proportion to the size of the drawer it is on. When matching pulls on doors and drawers, you may need to make some of them smaller even though they are the same style.

Another alternative is to cut the pulls into the face of the drawer. The possibilities are almost endless when you cut the pulls this way. Just make sure that no matter what you use for pulls, they fit in with the rest of the cabinet.

Hardware

Hardware is a necessary part of our craft. Often you can make or break a nice piece of furniture by the hardware you use. I tend to stick with tried and true when it comes to hardware, brass screws, butt hinges, knife hinges and brass and steel locks.

I make sure that the hardware is appropriate to the piece it is on and take plenty of time to fit it. Remember, before you make that first chisel cut, you can always change your mind.

Mounting Hardware

There are no tricks to getting a tight fit around your hardware. You do not have to go to elaborate lengths either. I use nothing more than marking tools and a sharp chisel. Careful marking and cutting are keys to a good fit. The one thing I usually do when mounting hardware is to cut the mortise slightly undersize when roughing it in and trim the edges to an exact fit as the last step. This gives me a gap free fit every time.

About Hinges

Hinges are, for the most part, simple. Two leaves connected to a pivot point. One leaf is attached to the carcase and the other to the door. The main thing you have to be sure of when mounting the hinge is that the center of the pivot is outside the plane of the door and carcase. Pay attention to this and your doors will work as planned every time, even on complex special purpose hinges.

Screws

Properly drilled pilot and shank holes will prevent broken screws. In ten years of making furniture the only reason I have broken screws is shoddy quality screws or the wrong pilot holes. I came across the following chart while I was at school and I am still grateful to the unknown individual who put it together. You will notice that it uses # drills and my advice is to get yourself a complete set (#1-60) of these bits.

Pilot and Shank Holes Chart

Screw	1	2	3	4	5	6	8	10
Shank Hole	48	43	39	33	29	28	17	10
Pilot Hole	53	52	48	45	40	38	31	25

If you really feel the need for further precautions run a steel screw of the same size into your pilot hole, as this will tap it for your finish screw.

I never bother to line up the slots in screws. It's one of those little details that no one (except other cabinetmakers) will ever see or notice and it also means you have to over tighten or loosen screws to make it happen. Screws have a primary purpose and that is mechanical, appearance comes secondary, but never in my mind at the expense of the first.

One other thing to consider when putting in screws, make sure that your screwdriver properly fits the screw head. If it doesn't, you are going to tear up the screw, the hardware or the cabinet it's going into. Don't be afraid to go to the grinder with your screwdrivers to make them fit screws properly, tight in the slot with no part of the blade sticking out of the side of the screw.

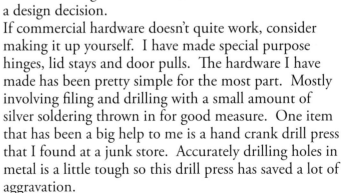

Choosing Hardware
Never let hardware change a design decision. If commercial hardware doesn't quite work, consider making it up yourself. I have made special purpose hinges, lid stays and door pulls. The hardware I have made has been pretty simple for the most part. Mostly involving filing and drilling with a small amount of silver soldering thrown in for good measure. One item that has been a big help to me is a hand crank drill press that I found at a junk store. Accurately drilling holes in metal is a little tough so this drill press has saved a lot of aggravation.

Unfortunately though, my experience is limited in this area so it would be foolish to try and teach you about metalworking. The best thing to do would be to take a metal working course or find a good book that clearly explains the process.

Before you jump out to buy specialty hardware, consider alternatives first. Bed bolts are a good example of this. Traditional bed bolts are expensive, and for the cost of only one of these, you can buy ordinary bolts from any hardware store that are entirely suitable and much more easily replaced in the event that one is lost.

Aging Brass

One of the things I picked up when I was at school was a technique to color brass. It is very simple to do. You need a large jar with something attached to the lid on which you can hang hinges and other hardware. I used two small eyebolts for mine.

First remove all finish from the brass you want to color. The finish will prevent this technique from working. 100 grit sandpaper works well for this. Fortunately, most of the hardware I buy has little to no finish on it.

Using Ammonia Fumes

Place a small amount of wood shavings in the bottom of the jar and pour in about a quarter cup of ordinary household ammonia. Attach the hardware to the lid with wire so the pieces you wish to color are hanging in the vapors, but not touching the shavings or the liquid ammonia. The next day your brass will have a nice "aged" look to it. Sometimes this can work in only a few hours, but I usually leave the hardware in the jar overnight.

When you remove the hardware from the jar rinse it off with water, then dry. Properly dispose of the ammonia and shavings (I used to flush them myself).

This method also works well for screws, but they may take longer to color as the brass used for screws is a harder alloy and reacts differently to the fumes. To make this easy, run your screws into a small block of wood that easily can be hung from the lid. One note of caution; this can cause stress cracks in brass, but I have only had this problem with cheap pressed hinges that I no longer use.

Finishing

I have been partial to oil finishes for years. I think they are the closest you can get to what fresh sawn wood might look like. Other finish types just look like plastic to me. I also really like how oil brings out the light and dark highlights of figured grain. Another benefit is the easy reparability by just about anyone.

Mixing Oil and Wax

I use an oil and wax mixture that I came across a few years ago and I have been very pleased with the results. The mixture is made up of 4 oz of beeswax, melted into a half gallon of boiled linseed oil. A half-gallon of oil goes a long way; so don't hesitate to mix up a smaller batch if that is all you need.

The best way to do this is to shred the wax into the oil, then heat the oil just enough to melt the wax. Do this outside, preferably over electric heat, as linseed oil is flammable. After the wax is completely dissolved you can pour the oil/wax mixture into smaller containers for storage and use. It will stay hot for a long time so make sure you don't seal up your container until it has cooled. I have found that Grolsch beer bottles are very handy for this purpose. Their resealable tops are tolerant of the oil that builds up around the neck while you use the contents, not to mention the fact that you get to empty the bottles in the first place....

As the mixture cools it will go from clear to a "cider" color and the wax will stay homogenized. You can use the mixture hot or cold, so you don't have to re-heat it each time you use it.

Applying an Oil Finish

Once you have your oil ready the next most important thing you need is rags, and lots of them. I use mostly lint free, old cotton napkins that I got from a commercial laundry; they usually sell them by the pound. And I also get more than one use by washing them, but only after they soak in a bucket of water. While they soak in the bucket add a little dish soap to help break down the oil.

You have heard this before and you are about to hear it again, oily rags are a hazard if just left around or directly thrown in the garbage. Don't. If you are going to throw them away, put them in a safe place to dry thoroughly before doing so.

And speaking of hazards, it is probably not a good idea to soak your hands in oil without some sort of protection, so get yourself some gloves. I use latex gloves from the pharmacy, no not the sterile kind, non-sterile are cheaper.

How Much Oil

I apply at least 3 coats, more if I have the time and inclination. Flood the first coat, put it on by brush or rag and let it soak for a half hour or so. Next, try and wipe off all the oil. Don't worry, you can't get it all, only the excess left on the surface will come off. Change your rags frequently as they get saturated with oil.

On the following coats the oil is used more like a polish. Apply a bit to a rag and rub it on. As the applicator rag gets dry, add a bit more oil and keep going. Cover the whole piece this way, then wipe off all you can with clean rags.

Something that old texts are very vague on is the fact that oil finishes are more rub than oil after the first coat. I think this is the key to a good oil finish, one part oil, twenty parts elbow grease and lots of fresh clean rags.

Things to Consider

Wait at least three days between coats, longer if possible. Sometimes this mixture can feel greasy, but it will go away on it's own in a couple of days.

Never oil the interior of a cabinet or drawer. I did oil the inside of my toolbox, but this box spends most of its life open to the air so it's not a problem. Linseed oil trapped inside a box is not a pleasant smell.

One thing you may find helpful is to keep a block and rag handy to clean up corners and narrow grooves. This works better than rags alone in these hard to get at areas.

Wax

I always apply a good coat or two of paste wax to a finished piece. Clapham's Beeswax Polish is my wax of choice for this. It goes on very easy and buffs out to a satin shine over the oil finish I use.

Waxing serves two purposes, it helps to prevent dents by helping objects glance off and it makes cleaning the piece easier. And no, the wax should not collect dirt unless it was applied way too heavily. The only time I ever had a problem with dirt was when I used wax as the only finish on some drawer fronts. They tended to get dirty around the finger pulls from frequent use. But when used over a finish, I have not had a problem.

I also apply wax to the interior of a cabinet. No really good reason for this, but do use a wax with a nice scent to it, floor type paste wax sometimes has quite an unpleasant odor after it dries. I

use Clapham's when I am doing the inside of a cabinet, but in drawer pockets I use floor wax, as it has a harder consistency. Some softer waxes will actually make a drawer harder to open. Also take a few swipes with a bar of paraffin along the running surface of drawers to help them glide smoothly and help to reduce wear.

Stains or Lack of Them

Stains have no place in my shop and unless you are totally callous in your wood selection they have next to no place in yours. Mother nature has been coloring wood for thousands of years and I don't think man has improved on her yet. If you want a different color, use a different wood.

Manufacturers substitute stain for careful attention to grain and color matching. Most people are completely surprised to learn that cherry has such wonderful colors and subtle grain patterns not the muddy mess of expensive mass-produced furniture from the major manufacturers.

Varnish

There are times when oil by itself is an inappropriate finish, such as exterior woodwork on boats and outdoor furniture. What I like to use whenever a piece needs to hold up to the weather is traditional varnish. It's available in either a glossy or a satin finish and with a bit of practice it is fairly simple to apply.

One of the things I like about varnish is that all you need to apply it is a brush and a fairly clean workspace. Fortunately, it is very forgiving of the environment it's used in. You would not believe some of the conditions I have seen varnish used in at the boatyard where I work and always with great results.

There are numerous manufacturers but I tend to stick to one maker when I need varnish, Epifanes. Someone told me that Epifanes was all I needed to know about varnish and this advice has held up very well. It's expensive, but cheap varnishes are just not worth the time and effort. You probably won't find it at the local hardware store but a boating supply store should have it.

Because I use varnish infrequently I prefer not to go into the details of how I apply it. There are others who can offer up better advice on how to use it. If you are thinking of giving varnish a try, look up some info in magazines and books on the particulars of how to put it on. There are books available that cover the subject in detail and occasional articles in Woodenboat can be very helpful. And don't overlook what's written on the can, you would be surprised with how much info is there.

For more info about a great product that comes out of Canada

Clapham's Beeswax Products Ltd.
324 Le Feuvre Rd
Abbotsford, British Columbia V4X 1A2
Canada
(800) 667-2939

And don't forget the website. www.claphams.com

Almost There...

     Even when you think you are done there is one more thing to do. Completion time is reflection time. A chance to look at what went right and what went wrong. (My Aunt once told me not to point out mistakes, sometimes you are the only one who can see them.) Think about what would you change and what you wouldn't.

     Take the time to look at your work and enjoy the results of your labor. Generally mistakes fade rapidly and are remembered only with effort, but the satisfaction of having done it all by hand lingers on....

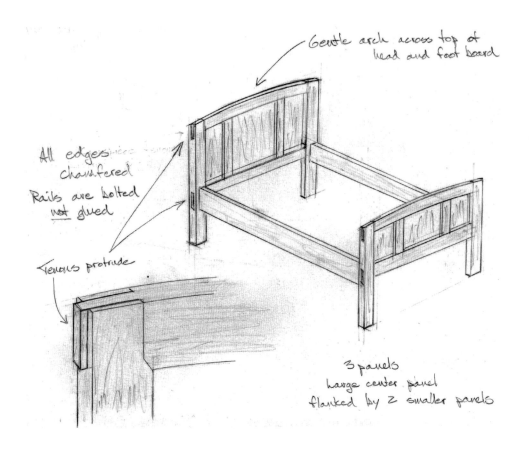

Gentle arch across top of
head and foot board

All edges
chamfered
Rails are bolted
not glued

Tenons protrude

3 panels
large center panel
flanked by 2 smaller panels

100

Drawings and Design

It doesn't matter how much of a master of your tools you are, if you do not have a good sense of design you are in trouble. But I do believe that this can be learned just like the technical skills used to make furniture.

Any discussion of design can get scary in a hurry. Good design for me can be put very simply, the object has to be well made, be pleasing to look at and it must have utility. Well made and utility are pretty easy to define, but pleasing to look at is where the fur starts to fly. Design is such a matter of personal taste, what is pleasing to one makes another gag. I think if you pay careful attention to the construction and the use of a piece, the appearance tends to follow along. Form follows function at its most basic. I don't know who gets the credit for this philosophy, but there is not a piece of my work that has not been made this way.

Compose as you go is an idea brought up by Jim Krenov in his books and while I tend to set up the entire piece in my head I do believe Jim's philosophy plays a part in how I build things.

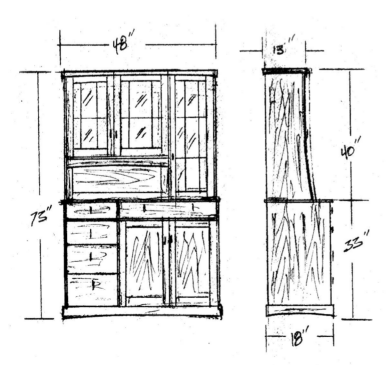

As I mentioned at the start of this book, you should not let the tools dictate just what it is you make, but this doesn't mean you should not let the tools have a say. Joinery and surface textures can be important elements to a design.

Another important element in how I make things is what I call working to fit not measurement. Parts of a cabinet are cut to fit an intended location, not to match a measurement on a drawing. This teaches you to be flexible while you are working, something that a mechanical drawing doesn't encourage. Altering one element can throw off an entire drawing, a problem that I don't have should I choose to alter some part of a cabinet. All I have to do is make sure everything fits as I work.

Attention to Detail

A lot of the nicest things about my cabinets are very subtle and most of them don't show in photographs, the fit of doors and drawers, how joinery is used and the feel of knobs and surfaces to name a few.

Paying attention to all of these things, both design and construction, helps make a better piece. Rather than one feature that stands out, it's the cabinet as a whole that you see. One nice thing leads to another.

About Drawings and Mock-ups

Only recently did I begin doing sketches and these are only for a clients benefit not mine. I make things all the time without drawings of any kind. I believe that mechanical drawings are overdoing it. Time spent drawing could be better spent building. You don't need every little dimension to get started. Most of the little stuff will settle itself.

I tend to build in my head before committing tools to wood or pencil to paper. I think through almost every detail, essentially building the piece in my head. What does help this is to stick to a certain style for your work and repeated details become second nature and don't need to be worked out on paper or with mock-ups.

And speaking of mock-ups, I do not like them. They take up a lot of time and are of little benefit to me. I think you should only use them sparingly to help train your eye in what to look for, proportion, shape, etc. or to help you work out some new or complex joinery. One thing to note is that I do not consider the patterns I use for curves to be mock-ups.

Proportion and Dimension

Don't overbuild. I think most of us have this problem when we first start making things. Door frames are too heavy, joinery is overdone or any number of little errors compounded by putting them all on the same piece.

When it comes to proportion and dimension, there is a boatbuilding adage that I think is very appropriate, add lightness and simplify...

I have a very simple philosophy for sizing my work; I make things in relationship to myself or a client and what they will be used for. Heights and widths etc. are all based on how they relate to me, the client or are fixed by an object going into the cabinet.

An Interesting Exercise

I learned an interesting lesson one day in the relationship between an idea and a finished piece of furniture. I was looking at the photo of a piece I had just finished and I noticed that the picture as usual didn't do justice to the piece. This made me break out the drawing, done to give a clear picture to the client, of the piece I was going to make for them. And what struck me was that even though the piece turned out exactly as I had planned, there was an interesting relationship between each step of the process. From idea to drawing to finished piece to photograph, there was a different image created at each step. Try it on one of your own pieces sometime.

17

58

TOTAL
27 HT

9½ CLEARENCE
FOR TRAIN

Some of My Work

I have never had a clear and concise explanation for why I work the way I do. The best answer I have is to point to my work. Let it stand on it's own merits and leave it up to you whether or not I am doing the right thing. I think I am.

The following pages show a few examples of my work and offers up some of the reasons for why I made them the way I did. The main reason I have included this section is so you can see some of the things I have made with the methods covered in the previous pages. In a way, it adds validity to my words and offers some justification for working with hand tools. The end results justify the tools used and time taken to achieve them.

Hopefully, these pages will provide some encouragement and inspiration for your own work with hand tools.

Alder China Cabinet

72H x 36W x 18D

This is the cabinet mentioned in the Carcase Joinery chapter that finally made its way to Norway. It was the first cabinet where I used a housed sliding

dovetail to hold two sections together.

The overall size of this cabinet came about in an interesting way. The client wanted a small china cabinet about as tall as me and the width was set by holding up my hands until a nice width was reached. Simple, but it worked. This is why I am a firm believer that you should build in relation to yourself.

When you make something that "feels" right, relative to "your" dimensions, the end result is usually a little easier to predict. It is still one of my favorite pieces.

Arch Top Blanket Chest

19H x 17D x 40W

The first piece of furniture I ever made was a blanket chest and they are still one of my favorite things to make. I think the reason for this is that the form is so basic and straightforward.

After making quite a few of these, my design sense started to wander and I wanted to add something more to them. I had made a few coopered panels so I figured it would add a nice detail, a gentle arching top, to an already pleasing cabinet. Coopering the top did make the lid rather complicated, but the end result is worth the effort.

The base trim has curves cut along the bottom to tie in to the curves of the top panel and trim of the lid.

Alder Books Cabinet

72H x 30W x 13D

      I tend to accumulate a lot of books and I wanted a nice place to keep them. I also wanted to see some of them so I decided on glass doors on the upper part of the cabinet.

I kept the cabinet small enough to be able to leave it in one piece, as I had just finished a large two-part cabinet and wanted things to be a little simpler for this case. But I did complicate things slightly when I put the gentle arch into the top of the doors.

Walnut Corner Cabinet

21H x 16W x 9D

    At first glance this cabinet is very unassuming. Upon taking a closer look things get a bit more complicated. The solid back panel makes a 90-degree bend from one side to the other. The back panel is coopered to make this curve and rides in a groove to accommodate movement.

    Because the bend of the panel is next to impossible to clamp up for gluing, all of the joints were "rubbed", which eliminates the need for clamps during glue up. My pipe clamp vise was indispensable while I made this cabinet. I also made special brackets to hang this cabinet that allow the solid top and bottom to expand and contract.

    While I have to admit this cabinet has limited use, it was a lot of fun to make.

Alder Cupboard Chest

67H x 34W x 18D

I have made several of these cabinets and each time I make little changes. Mostly minor improvements, but the one thing I have never altered is the overall size. I guess you have to get lucky and hit something just right once in awhile.

This is also the piece where I learned how important it is to graduate the sizes of the drawers. Each level of the drawers varies by 1", starting at 5" at the top and finishing with 9" at the bottom.

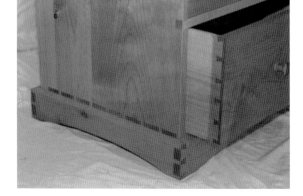

Pear Letters Box   3H x 12L x 9W

The main idea behind this box was the desire to conceal as much of the joinery as possible. The main part of the box is held together with full blind dovetails and to help take your eye off the joinery of the lid, it is put together with an open bridle joint that is mitered on the outside surface.

Due to how I made this box I had to make special hinges. I also made the lid stay and knobs. All of the brass hardware has been colored with ammonia fumes to darken it and eliminate the shine of new brass.

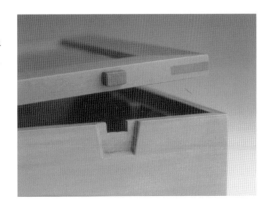

The other major influence on this box was my dislike of phones. I would much rather answer a letter than a phone.

Alder Library Cabinet

75H x 61W x 19D

    This piece was the first piece I made that I looked to my own work for inspiration rather than the work of others. The original request from the client was for a cabinet twice the size of the Books Cabinet seen a few pages earlier.

    The panels in the lower doors had a say in things as well. I only had one 10 ft piece of Alder, 13" wide, with the birds' eye figure. What makes this special is that I have only seen this figure in Alder once in the thousands of board feet I have used or sorted through.

Trestle Table

84L x 36W x 30H

I really like the simplicity of trestle tables. One large flat surface, two "I" shaped legs and a stretcher to tie them together. To soften things up on the eye there is a gentle arch at the bottom of the stretcher and subtle curves on the edges of the top.

One really nice thing about trestle tables is the knockdown feature, all it takes is a hammer to take one apart or put it together when you have to move it.

Walnut China Cabinet

75H x 50W x 18D

There are a few things that influenced this design. The idea for an asymmetrical layout came from an Art Nouveau piece I had seen in a book. I had also done a sideboard similar to the bottom half of this cabinet. The overall size is about the same as a hutch my mom has had since I was a kid, and the gentle curves in the base frame, along the top of the upper doors, and other places came about from a desire to soften the rectilinear lines I am partial to.

The Shaker ideal of function first has certainly found its way into this piece. There is no applied ornamentation or things that do not need to be there.

Once I had the design figured out, I had to get the wood. Walnut was my first choice all along with one problem, no money. Simple solution, sell my truck. So even the wood had some say on the outcome.

Alder Sweater Cabinet

64H x 46W x 18D

This cabinet was made to hold nothing but sweaters. The shelves in the upper section and the bottoms of the drawers are all made of eastern red cedar to hopefully keep the moths away. The use of an extra stile in the doors allowed me to use some interesting wood for the panels and keep the panel size in proportion to the rest of the door

Due to it's size this cabinet was made in two pieces that are held together with a housed sliding dovetail.

Sooz Sewing Box

16W x 12D x 4½H

Mahogany and Purpleheart

I made this box as a present to my wife. It holds all of her cross-stitch supplies or at least it was intended to until I found out just how many colors of floss are available.

The outer box and tray are mahogany and the panel in the lid, lid handles and interior dividers are all of Purpleheart. You might notice that the dovetails are tapered although the exterior of the box is still square.

The hinges are handmade and the lid stay is made of embroidery floss. The lock is not for security but rather to keep out the fingers of our boys when they were of a much younger age.

Books to Have

The following list is what I think would form a good library for a hand tool woodworker. I have quite a few more books than this but these are the ones I would not want to do without.

Encyclopedia of Furniture Making, Ernest Joyce, 1970
> Get the unrevised edition from a used bookstore. The new version is not very well done. All they did to revise this classic was to change the order of the chapters and add some color pictures and in doing so they made it rather confusing to read

Modern Practical Joinery, George Ellis, Reprint of 1908 edition
> Available from many catalogs or direct from Linden Publishing

The Practical Woodworker and The Complete Woodworker
> Reprints from Ten Speed Press. Two nice books from the turn of the century well worth having.

Adventures in Wood Finishing, George Frank, 1981
> The Taunton Press. Just a fun read.

Dictionary of Woodworking Tools, R.A. Salaman, 1975
> Reprint available from The Astragal Press. Covers just about every woodworking tool ever made or thought of, even a neat way to make a hat.

The Workbench Book, Scott Landis, 1987
> The Taunton Press, worth every penny.

The Unknown Craftsman, Soetsu Yanagi, 1972
> Kodansha International, A sometimes hard to read book, but it should be on your shelf.

Welsh Stick Chairs, John Brown, 1990
> The author's attitude and approach to chairs makes this worth having.

The Making of Tools, Alexander G. Weygers, 1973
> You will probably have to find this one at a used bookstore. I have also heard that Ten Speed Press has a reprint.

Planecraft, Hand Planing by Modern Methods, C. W. Hampton and E. Clifford, 1934
> Try Woodcraft Supply to find this one. I believe they are the publishers of the reprints.

Keeping the Cutting Edge, Harold H. Payson, 1983
> Woodenboat Publications, You need this book to learn how to sharpen saws.

The Woodwrights Eclectic Workshop, Roy Underhill, 1991
> University of North Carolina Press. I like all of Roy Underhill's books, but this one is worth having if for nothing more than the introduction.

All of Jim Krenov's books

My Tools and Toolbox

A toolbox is so much more than a place to keep your tools. I am a firm believer that your toolbox should be a reflection of your skills and the type of work you are capable of. It can even serve as a sample of your work if you put enough time and effort into it. A painted box just wasn't in the cards for me....

I use a traditional toolbox

to hold virtually all of my tools. It is placed less than a step away from my bench for easy and convenient access. Tools are removed on an as needed basis, use it then put it away. There is no reason to leave it out if you are not using it.

I once heard someone criticize this type of box because they felt it required too much stooping and bending to get at the contents. My only question for them is, why are they a woodworker if they don't like stooping and bending?

At first glance my toolbox seems overly complex and people often wonder how I ever made it. I have to admit like a lot of things, it evolved with my needs. It was not the first tool chest I built, rather it is a refinement of two others I had previously made. The first was laid out wrong and the second had so many changes it was time to make a new one. And like the others, this box was designed from the inside out, the contents made most of the important decisions.

There are over 400 tools in my chest and everything has a place. I can see at a glance if something is out of place or missing. Everything is available with a minimum need to move something else. I can get to anything quickly, with my eyes closed if need be. Accessibility of tools was the problem with my first chest.

Tool Box Layout

I like using a traditional chest, but I did make a few changes of my own to make it a little more usable. The tills inside the chest are laid out in a side-to-side arrangement rather than front to back. Front to back tills don't work very well. I can't explain just why cabinetmakers of the past did not think of this, as a side-to-side layout is far more practical and efficient. None of the trays and tills have lids. Lids look nice, but they are only a nuisance when I am working.

There are two small removable boxes between the tills that are removed when I start work and put back at the end of the day. One of the boxes holds all of my drills and the other holds assorted odds and ends.

All of my saws fit behind or on a hinged panel attached to the lid. To keep the heavy lid from tearing the hinges out I added two hinged supports to the back of the chest that allow the lid to lean back slightly.

While you could call my box portable, it must be partially emptied in order to

move it. It weighs in excess of 300 lbs so it takes four men and a boy to lift. I did install handles but these mostly get used to shift it around on the floor when needed.

More Than a Box
I use my toolbox for more than just tool storage; it is also an example of my work. A business card of sorts and a place to show people just what I am capable of.

There are numerous types of wood in my toolbox. The majority of it is made of Walnut and Alder, but you will also find Holly, Manzanita, Pear, Pine, Ebony, Bloodwood, Maple, Quilted Maple, Cherry, Yellow Cedar, Douglas Fir, Mahogany, Jarrah and Purpleheart.

I carved my name and a Latin saying into the inner lid with a chip carving knife and there is over 73 feet of 1/16" stringing inlaid in various places. The stringing is made of Holly, Pear, Walnut and Manzanita. If you want to know what the latin means, look up Hippocrates, he's the guy who said it….

As for this last pic it shows how the lid is supported when open and also should

give you an idea of why I used the wood I did.

There are over 400 hours of labor in this chest and I don't know if it will ever really be done. I often find little things I want to do and there is still a bit of carving I haven't done yet....

However you make your chest, do it right.

Mistakes, even if others can't see them, are very apparent to you when you work out of it every day.

What's in my Toolbox?

The following is a list of pretty much everything contained in my toolbox and shop. I include this list with a word of advice. Don't look at it as a must have list. There is no such thing. I bought my tools over a period of about 5 years as I found a need for each one. Do the same and your kit will be totally suited to what you make.

Chisels

7 Bench chisels 1/8" to 1" by 1/8ths
7 Registered mortise chisels 1/2" to 1 1/2"
Crank neck chisel 1/2"
1/4" Lock Mortise chisel
3/8" Bench chisel ground thin for tight spots
set of 37 carving chisels (at last count)

6 Sash mortise chisels 3/16" to 1/2"
Patternmakers chisel 1/2"
In-cannel gouge
2 handmade chisels for keyholes

Mallets and Hammers

10 oz Warrington
10 oz claw
Large wooden mallet
4 nail sets

3 oz Warrington
12 oz Blacksmith
Round wooden mallet

Planes

#07 jointer
#90 Bullnose
#073 Shoulder Rabbet
#95 Edging Plane
3 Round bottom planes
#71 Router
Wood rabbet plane w/fence
#45 Combination plane

#04 Smoother
#93 Shoulder Rabbet
#79 Side Rabbet
Chisel Plane
Low angle block plane
#271 Router
Dovetail plane
#05 Jackplane with curved blade

Saws

28" Rip 4tpi
12" Tenon 15tpi
21" Panel lltpi 5"
Piercing (jewelers saw)
Bow saw
Dado saw
Veneer saw

24" Crosscut 8tpi
8' Dovetail 20tpi
Bead saw 36tpi
Coping (mostly 15tpi blades)
Straight handle backsaw with depth gauge
Fretsaw (same blades as Piercing saw)

Spokeshaves
#151 flat sole
Kunz adjustable throat spokeshave
3 small detail spokeshaves
Spare blades for all planes and spokeshaves

Drills
12" Brace
3 Forstner bits 1/2", 3/4", 1"
2 Egg beater drills
4 Brad point bits
Yankee push drill with 8 bits
16 dowel points
3/8 Jacobs chuck with handle
Brace extension
1/4" x 12" bit
Set of fractional bits 1/16" to 1/4" by 64ths

13 brace bits 1/4" to 1" by 16ths
Adjustable expansive bit
Set of # drill bits 1 to 60
5 counter sinks (2 to fit brace)
2 drill gauges (# and fractional)
screw gauge
2 pin vises for small bits
3/8" x 18" Bellhangers bit

Screw Drivers
4 straight slot
Crutch pattern straight slot
set of jewelers

3 Phillips
2 straight slot for planes
Slotted bit for saw handles

Sharpening Stuff
2 ceramic stones, fine and coarse
Coarse carborundum
Soft Arkansas
Hard Black Arkansas
Auger bit file
Oil can
2 saw sets, coarse and fine
roller guide for chisels and narrow blades

7 ceramic files
Washita
Hard White Arkansas
brush for cleaning stones
Various taper files for saws
8x lens
angle gauge
strop

Knives
mill knife
chip carving knife
sheeps foot carving knife
utility knife

2 curved blade knives for carving
detail knife
12" drawknife
pocketknife

Files and Rasps

#49 pattern rasp
10" cabinet rasp
10" cabinet file
6" mill bastard
8" round file
6" half round file

#50 pattern rasp
10" round rasp
8" cabinet file
10" round file
6" round file
12 needle files

Tapes and Rules

12" bi-fold rule
24" bi-fold rule
6" metal rule

12' tape
72" folding rule

Marking and Measuring Tools

scratch awl
8" square
5"double square
depth gauge
compass
6" level
brass plumb bob
center punch

bent scratch awl
adjustable pattern square
2 marking/mortise gauges
winding sticks
stair gauges
spar gauge
pair of trammel points

Scrapers

#80 cabinet scraper
1" hook scraper with Teak handle
triangular burnisher

5 flat cabinet scrapers various thicknesses
scratch beader with 8 blades

Odds and Ends

Tweezers
small mirror
roll of blue masking tape
putty knife
sandwich picks for gluing dowel holes
2 sliding T-bevels, 5" and 12"
protractor
dividers
panel gauge
pencils
spring loaded center punch
large glue brush

chalk
crescent wrench
palette knife for spreading glue
beam for trammel points
toothbrush and small brush for wax
butt mortise gauge
mullet block
framing square
24" straight edge
calipers
lipstick for marking hardware
chalk line

vise grips
wire cutters

small glue brush
bar of paraffin

Shop Tools
    The first part of this list has all been tools that are kept in my toolbox. The following are just as important but don't fit in the box.

4' metal rule/straight edge
8 spring clamps
20 5" C-clamps
assorted Curve patterns
Clamping blocks
Hand Grinder and dressing wheel
Propane torch
Hardware cabinet (hinges and screws)
Glass lapping plate
Bucket of clean rags
Panel stop
Pan for heating oil mixture
Joinery samples
Pencil Sharpener

72" level
40 pipe clamps
6 2" C-clamps
Glue bottle
Saw Filing Vise
Metal working vise
Hand crank Drill Press
First Aid Kit
Jar for Fuming Brass
Bench hook
Small vise mounted bench
Radio
Board jack

Making a Living and Formal Training

I hesitated to include this chapter but it would be irresponsible on my part not to address these concerns and share some of my experiences. I would like to add some words of wisdom, the following is my own feelings about these matters and I speak for no one else. Your own experience could be totally different.

Woodwork as a Job

It is not easy to earn a living making furniture. Money was never my guiding light and to be perfectly honest, I don't have an easy answer to this one. What has been of equal importance to me, besides making money, is the desire to make a life. To have time for family and friends and other things in life besides work. Making a dream (some might say fantasy) come true is not the easiest thing to do, especially with 3 young boys in the house.

I am making a living from my woodwork but not from making furniture. I have been working as the lead yacht carpenter in small boat yards for the last 15 years or so.

I turned to boats not because I wanted to change direction but to pay the bills. It's interesting work but I don't want to do it forever. Interestingly enough a portfolio of my cabinetwork is what got me the job in the first place. I have also worked in a lumberyard and drove a laundry truck to pay the bills during slow periods of little to no sales. I have not given up on making furniture for a living nor do I intend to either.

Selling Your Work

Find your niche and stay within it. If you like to make simple, elegant things, as I do, don't step out and try to do Queen Anne. At least don't just do it for the money. Doing it for the challenge or experience is another matter. Building a reputation takes a long time and a lot of work.

Don't work under the table. I have found that most people who want me to work this way are cheap. They want me to work at a reduced price and help them avoid paying the sales tax. In reality you are breaking the law and the only person who benefits is the purchaser. One other thing, if it's not on your tax return the bank doesn't consider it income and that money could get you a needed loan, for a house or maybe for some needed shop improvements.

Don't work at a loss. You should not take a job that directly costs you money.

You would be far better off making a piece on speculation than losing money from the get go.

If you make things just for the money you will get customers who aren't coming to you for what you really want to do. If you are consistently the low bidder you might always attract people who want the lowest price rather than the high quality and uniqueness of your work. Set a fair price for your work and stick with it.

Word of Mouth

This is absolutely the best sales tool I have. It has accounted for almost every sale I have ever made and it has been the main source of serious enquiries about my work that I have received.

Prompt replies to any inquiries generates some very good word of mouth advertising. I don't know how many times I have heard people complain about the lack of a response from a business or an individual. When someone has to hound you to get a reply they are not very likely to recommend you to anyone. Bad service will get you nowhere.

Going the Extra Mile

I like to be involved in the entire sale, all the way from picking out the wood to delivering the piece in a trailer I bought just for this purpose. Delivery and set up of a finished piece in a customer's home makes for some great word of mouth referrals. If you are going to do this you have to have a decent way to deliver things. I fought this for years  before I bought the trailer I have now. It has tie downs galore and also holds lumber purchases out of the weather, very important here in the Northwest where I live.

Promoting Your Work

Writing technical articles about your work can be fun and interesting and it can also earn you a bit of extra money, but you are not going to get rich doing it. Nor is it going to generate much interest in your work from possible customers. Virtually every inquiry I have gotten from these articles has been people with questions of a technical nature. Asking how I do something or if plans are available, I answer the questions as best I can and no, I don't work from plans.

Most of the people I know who write about working wood for a living have next to no time to actually pick up their tools and make something or even much time to fiddle around in their shop.

The other possibility is articles about you and your work that are more special interest, rather than of a technical nature. But I have not had much luck in getting magazines to do a feature article no matter how interesting I try to make things. And just how effective this is, is open for debate. I have had articles written about me and the response has been lukewarm at best.

Write a book, I did.

A Modern Portfolio

No matter how good your work is, you are going to need pictures to show to customers. The pictures don't need to be of studio quality but they should give potential clients a very good idea of what you are capable of.

I used to have a portfolio but now with the magic of the internet I have it all on a website, tonykonovaloff.com. This saves me from having to mail out copies of the portfolio or other printed information. All I need to do now is send them the website address for much more info than I could ever provide in the four copies of my old portfolio that I used to keep on hand. The website shows much of my past work and includes quite a few words about my work and where I am going with it.

It's easy to keep updating the photographs as I make new pieces or do something interesting that's worth showing to others. What makes this easy to deal with is a digital camera and my computer. And as long as your photo's are already in your computer you can even come up with a simple or complex brochure easily if that is what you prefer.

These days the only paper I print is my business cards and even this I do on my computer. My cards include contact info and the address of my website as I know they are not going to remember how to spell my last name.

And don't forget that anything you put out is a reflection of you and your work.

Samples

You need to have samples of your work on hand at all times. And no, I am not talking about give aways. I am talking about full size pieces of your work. I don't know how many times people have asked to see a piece I have made after seeing a picture. Photo's are needed as well but they can't compare to being able to touch a finished piece. Since my shop is part of the house I just use the pieces that are in my house for this.

Samples of joinery are good to have around as well. Some of the things you do everyday can be extremely interesting to a potential customer. Joints that are not glued can make for interesting conversation starters.

You should also have wood and finish samples around as well. Just because you are around it everyday doesn't mean that your potential client knows what Alder or Walnut looks like. It drives me crazy when I show someone a picture of a Walnut piece and they ask what kind of stain that is.

Never underestimate the power of touch.

Galleries

I have dealt with galleries in California, Oregon and Washington and for one reason or another I have not had good luck selling my work through them. I cannot blame the staff at any of them for I did have some strong supporters of my work, but they just could not sell my work. Prices were in line with everyone else and I don't make really freaky stuff so I don't have a good explanation for the lack of sales. Galleries work for some people they just didn't work out for me.

Before you jump on the gallery bandwagon, take a long, hard and well thought out look before you commit to selling your work through them.

See how they will present your work. Take a look around at things similar to yours and see how it is displayed, if they are buried under other things they will never sell. How much knowledge does the staff have about cabinets and such? A lack of knowledge on their part could cost you a sale. Just what percentage of the price do they keep as a commission? Around 40 percent (or more…) is typical. Much too high in my book for a store that never purchases your work, but only provides display space for it.

There is a relationship between the gallery and the cabinetmaker that is the same as the one between the flea and the dog. A dog doesn't need fleas to survive. The galleries have got it backwards. They take an unusually large percentage of the price as a commission and act as if you can't exist without them. The reality of the situation is that the gallery cannot exist without you. You are the dog, without you there is no gallery. Don't forget this.

One other big reason I have gotten away from galleries is that I don't like the lack of contact with the person who buys my work. And I have to be honest, with one exception; I've never sold a piece to someone that has not met me.

Teaching Classes

Be brutally honest with yourself, not everyone can teach. We all have our faults when it comes to showing others how to do things and even though I think that I write things out pretty well, it doesn't make me a good teacher.

Classes can be a lot of fun, especially if you like to talk as much as I do. Pretty much everyone who is there is interested in learning how you do things. They are predisposed to how you work and what you have to say. And this can create some good word of mouth advertising for you as well.

Make sure to tailor the class to the students. See what their skill level is and just what it is they want to learn. It's no use showing them your fancy new mortise and tenon when all they want to do is cut dovetails. In your first couple of classes go in with an open mind and be ready to change things around to suit the situation.

130

Formal Training

This is a big gray area. I had been working as an independent cabinetmaker for about 5 years before I went to school. The year I spent at school was both good and bad for me. In retrospect I think a full time school would be the most help for someone who doesn't have a whole lot of knowledge and bad habits. There are alternatives to school that can be just as good if not better.

I think the best thing you can do is to find a mentor. Someone to ask questions of and to get advice from. Preferably another woodworker, one who's work you like or works the way you want to. Working with handtools, this is not the easiest thing to find. Joining a local woodworkers association would be a good start to finding a mentor. Even if you don't find anyone like this, you will meet quite a few fellow woodworkers who have a lot in common with you.

Take short classes and workshops. Get the best from a class and then take it back to your own shop and put it to use. And don't show up to one of these classes thinking you are going to impress any one, you are there to learn, not to teach. Teaching comes later.

Read a lot. Pay attention to what others have to say. Listening to them doesn't mean you have to slavishly copy or emulate them, but you will learn from them.

School

If your heart is set on a full time school there are some things to consider before you choose one. Most importantly, plan on making a visit to the school. This will tell you a lot about the staff and the school. Ask a lot of questions of current students and the staff. Be sure that the school and instructors are on the same plane as you. Don't assume that the school has the same goals as you. Don't forget to take account of the cost of attending; are you going to be able to recover the money spent to attend?

See what the mix of students is. Most of the people in your class should have the same basic skill level. If there is a broad range of skills in the same class, this makes for a very difficult blend to teach.

One thing I have to give credit to College of the Redwoods is that they were very family friendly, or at least were when I was there. I frequently had my oldest son with me and he had a great time at my bench or when he moved over to Cecilia's bench which is where he is in that picture.

Lastly, take a good look at what it is the school doesn't teach. Do they bring in outsiders to talk about subjects they don't cover or are unable to teach, such as the business side of things? The things they don't cover could be of more importance to you than the things they do.

Business How-to Books

Growing a Business, Paul Hawken, 1987, Simon and Schuster
Marketing Without Advertising, Michael Phillips and Salli Rasberry, 1986, Nolo Press
Small Time Operator, Bernard Kamaroff, 1988, Bell Springs Publishing

Glossary

We all have our own vocabulary and way of using terms. This list, hopefully, will give you some insight into mine.

ABC

awl - sharpened and used properly, a very accurate marking tool
bit - unit of measurement, see smidgen
back panel - frame and panel that serves as the back of a carcase
back saw - a small saw with a stiffener fitted along the top edge of the saw
baseline - the mark you don't cut beyond
batten - a stick used to mark a line or guide a tool
bench hook - a small board that hooks the edge of your bench and is fitted with a stop for cross cutting small pieces and other assorted tasks
bevel - an angle cut on the edge of a board
blow out - when wood tears out at the back while planing end grain or working across the grain of a board
board jack - holds up the end of long boards
brace - the handle used with auger bits and other large cutting bits
break an edge - taking out the sharpness on the edges of a chamfer
bridle joint - an open type of mortise and tenon
burnish - using various materials to polish up a surface or edge, also how you create the hooked edge of a scraper
cabinetmaker - maker of fine furniture
cap iron - the piece of metal screwed to the blade of an iron bench plane
carborundum - manmade abrasive, a mix of carbon and silicon
carcase - the main part of a cabinet, minus doors, drawers, trim, etc.
chamfer - small flat, cut on the edges of cabinets
clean up - removing excess glue or wood, initial flattening or straightening
coopered - putting boards together so they form a curved panel
cupping - the tendency of the rings of a tree to straighten out once it is cut into a board
cut list - a thing I don't use because I cut things out only as I need them

DEF

dado - a groove that runs across the grain of a board or panel
depth - how deep a hole is or the front to back measurement of a cabinet
diagonals - used to check the squareness of a carcase, door, etc.

Disston - at one time, the maker of the best handsaws available

drawer blade - a frame that a drawer rides on, possibly of English origin

dry fit - clamping everything together without glue

edge - narrow part of boards or the business part of blades and chisels

elbow grease - what you use to get anything done with hand tools

end grain - type of grain, crosscut a board and take a look

escapement - concealed part of a knockdown joint that allows it to come apart

exposed joinery - joinery that is not hidden or concealed

eyeball - little thing in your face, trust it

face - the side that shows or the wide flat part of a board

figure - mostly used to describe unusual or wild grain

fit - how well something goes into its intended location

flat - a thing chased but rarely achieved, sort of like perfection

frog - the part of a metal plane that holds the blade assembly in place

GHI

glue block - a small block glued into a corner to strengthen it, generally rubbed

glue up - final assembly with glue

go bars - narrow sticks longer than the opening they are put into, use to force apart that opening or to hold things down

grain - what the wood looks like, the direction it's going or the type

guesstimate - trusting your eyes to cut and mark when practical

hooped - metal rings used on chisel handles to prevent them from splitting

honing - the final step in sharpening your edges

JKL

joinery - any thing used to put two pieces of wood together

jointer - a long soled plane used for edge jointing and flattening

kit - an English term for the collection of tools you use

kerf - the wood removed by your saw

lapping plate - flat surface used for initial flattening of planes, blades and chisels

layout - another way to say marking out

lever cap - the part of a metal plane that holds down the blade and cap iron

MNO

mallet - a wooden hammer used to pound on chisels

mill marks - saw and planer marks left by machines

mortise - the female side of a mortise and tenon

mullet block - a gauge block used to check the thickness of an edge *miter* - the angle, other than a right angle, where two surfaces meet, usually 45 degrees

open time - the amount of time you have before the glue takes a set

PQR

pare - using a chisel to shave off wood

pins - the narrow part of a dovetail that fits between the tails

piston fit - a sliding fit with no extra room or slop

plow - to cut a groove with the grain of a piece of wood

rabbet - a notch taken out of the edge or end of a piece of wood

rail - the horizontal member of a frame

rasp - similar to a file but with much coarser teeth to cut wood quickly

rip - cutting a board along its length

roughed out - an unfinished surface or edge

rubbed joint - edge joinery that uses no clamps

STUV

saw set - a tool used to bend the teeth on your saws

scribe line - a mark left by an awl, knife or marking gauge

scrub plane - a plane with a curved blade that takes a heavy cut

set - prior to fully curing, glue takes an initial set

shooting - using a plane on its side to ensure accuracy

shoulder - part of a tenon that sticks above the surface of the tenon

smidgen - see bit

smoother - a short-soled plane used to finish the surface of a board

spur cutters - small blades that sever the grain ahead of the main blade when cutting cross grain with some types of planes, mainly rabbet and combination planes

square - a relative term, close enough is sometimes appropriate

squeeze out - the glue that comes out of a joint during clamp up

stile - the vertical member of a frame

stones - rocks used for sharpening. They are mined in an area of Arkansas, hence the name Arkansas stones

stop - a block of wood or screw used to keep a piece of wood from sliding around when it is being worked on

stringing - narrow strips of wood inlaid for decoration

tails - the wider part of dovetails

tang - the tapered part of a file meant for attaching a handle

taper - a board that gets thinner across its width or length

temper - the final hardness of a blade or chisel

tenon - the male part of a mortise and tenon joint

throat - the opening in the sole of a plane where the shavings pass through

tills -   open trays and boxes in a toolbox
trim -   parts not integral to the carcase

WXYZ

wane -   the bark edge left on a board after it is sawn from a log
warrington - a style of hammer
winding sticks - used to find twist or wind

End of the Book Say So

My kids have grown up quite a bit since I first wrote this but if you have young kids you may find that it is very appropriate. Besides I just love these old pics of my boys when they were still shorter than me.

Like a lot of folks I found balancing family and shop time was not the easiest thing to do. Fortunately my boys enjoyed being

in the shop with me and with rare exception did I ever have to chase them out. Mostly this has to do with how I work. I have never been able to explain just why I work entirely by hand but when Benjamin, Jeremiah and Caleb were with me, I am thankful that I do.

Early on they learned just what they can and cannot pull out of my toolbox, chisels are a no-no, hammers, tapes etc. are OK and the putty knife is popular. It does not matter what I am working on whether planing boards, cutting dovetails or chopping mortises they were welcome to be there with little danger to body parts or health.

What was the biggest surprise to me though is how easily they fell asleep at my feet regardless of how much noise I was making. I guess they found my shop a pretty peaceful place when they were much younger.

Nowadays, they have their own bench and wood supply which keeps them occupied most of the time. Occasionally they will pester me beyond belief but I think this is just because they are kids.

Besides, I don't think I could

keep my shadow, Caleb, out of the shop for anything. If I was in the shop so was he.

And if this is not reason enough to keep working with hand tools I don't know what is.

Today my boys have all gotten quite a bit bigger. The two oldest, Benjamin and Jeremiah, are now taller than I am and the youngest, Caleb is well on track to passing me by as well. Part of me really hopes they decide to work with wood after they sort through the first part of their lives. But they all need to make their own decisions. I know I did.

The end and reward of toil is rest.

James Beattie

About the Author

I have been making furniture since 1986 when I made a Hope chest for my little sister and I guess you could say I got carried away from there. I made a decision very early on to work only with hand tools and I have never regretted it. Just why I made this decision, may take my lifetime to understand or explain.

I am self-taught mainly due to the fact that any sort of apprenticeship program, of the sort that were around at the turn of the century, no longer exists. After making furniture on my own for about five years, I did have the opportunity to attend the woodworking program at the College of the Redwoods in Ft. Bragg, CA. While, overall the year at school was a mixed blessing, there are a few things I picked up and continue to use to this day.

The biggest influence on my work would have to be the Shakers. They worked in a way that put function above all else, but at the same time gave objects a simple beauty. There is no applied ornamentation or things that do not need to be there. Nothing to take away and nothing to add. Other influences include Greene and Greene, Edward and Sidney Barnsley, Jim Krenov, John Brown, Roy Underhill and many others

The current state of the furniture industry as a whole has certainly affected the way that I make and design furniture. With the use of so much plywood, stains and machine techniques, the cabinetmaker is becoming lost in the shuffle. He (or she) is becoming an operator of machines and nothing more. I believe by using only hand tools, solid wood, traditional joinery and making pieces one at a time, I am putting the maker back into a piece of furniture.

A lot of myself goes into each and every piece of furniture I make, and it shows. I really care about what I do, not only the end result, but also in how it gets done. There is a quiet dignity to my work and I think you will agree.

Why hand tools? Mainly because I enjoy it. Also, hand tools have become a sign of quality unhurried, reminiscent of a time when very different attitudes prevailed.

Cabinets, Pencils and Wood

I started writing about working wood just before I went to school. I wrote about my toolbox for Fine Woodworking magazine and this lead to other articles about my work and how I do things. I have had several articles published in Fine Woodworking and a piece of my furniture was featured in the now defunct Home Furniture magazine. I've also had an article printed in a British magazine, Good Woodworking, that is about my philosophy rather than a how-to.

While I have had some success with my writing, I would much rather be in my shop making a piece of furniture either to keep or to sell. For now, the only way I sell my work is through word of mouth. While this has been a tough road to hoe, in the end, I believe it will pay off.

Presently I live with my wife, Susan and two of my boys, Jeremiah and Caleb in the Pacific Northwest. Our oldest, Benjamin is off serving in the US Air Force.

Notes and such.

Yep it's OK to write on these last few pages….

Slowing down makes any journey less of a blur….

More Notes

In any contest between power and patience, bet on patience

W.B. Prescott

Even More Notes

Dedication and commitment to purpose is a solitary pursuit....

145

Where to get your own copy of this book

I have a couple of ways to make it easier for you. Go directly to my website www.tonykonovaloff.com and find the link to the book (It has a paypal option) or send me an email and I will help you get one, tonykonovaloff@hotmail.com

Or even ask your friendly bookstore to order it for you. All they should need is the ISBN number on the copyright page.